W9-DDR-571

The Elderly

Other books in the Current Controversies series:

The Elderly

Tamara Thompson, Book Editor

GREENHAVEN PRESS

An imprint of Thomson Gale, a part of The Thomson Corporation

THOMSON

━━━━━━✦━━━━━━ ™

GALE

Detroit • New York • San Francisco • San Diego • New Haven, Conn.
Waterville, Maine • London • Munich

Bonnie Szumski, *Publisher*
Helen Cothran, *Managing Editor*

© 2006 Thomson Gale, a part of The Thomson Corporation.

Thomson and Star Logo are trademarks and Gale and Greenhaven Press are registered trademarks used herein under license.

For more information, contact:
Greenhaven Press
27500 Drake Rd.
Farmington Hills, MI 48331-3535
Or you can visit our Internet site at http://www.gale.com

LIBRARY OF CONGRESS CATALOGING-IN-PUBLICATION DATA

The Elderly / Tamara Thompson, book editor
   p. cm. -- (Current controversies)
  Includes bibliographical references (p.) and index.
  0-7377-2781-0 (lib. : alk. paper) 0-7377-2782-9 (pbk. : alk. paper)
   1. Older people--United States--Social conditions--21st century. 2. Older people--Medical care--United States. 3. Social security--United States.
4. Privatization--United States. I. Thompson, Tamara. II. Series. (San Diego, Calif.)
  HQ1064.U5E3965 2006
  305.260973'09051--dc22
                                  2005055067

Printed in the United States of America
10 9 8 7 6 5 4 3 2 1

Contents

Chapter 2: Does Health Care Meet the Needs of the Elderly?

of the program. Privatization violates the spirit of Social Security.

Chapter 4: What Challenges Do the Elderly Face?

Communities often do not consider the needs of the elderly when they design public spaces. Offering accessible public transportation and safe walking routes can help the elderly remain independent.

Foreword

By definition, controversies are "discussions of questions in which opposing opinions clash" (Webster's Twentieth Century Dictionary Unabridged). Few would deny that controversies are a pervasive part of the human condition and exist on virtually every level of human enterprise. Controversies transpire between individuals and among groups, within nations and between nations. Controversies supply the grist necessary for progress by providing challenges and challengers to the status quo. They also create atmospheres where strife and warfare can flourish. A world without controversies would be a peaceful world; but it also would be, by and large, static and prosaic.

The Series' Purpose

The purpose of the Current Controversies series is to explore many of the social, political, and economic controversies dominating the national and international scenes today. Titles selected for inclusion in the series are highly focused and specific. For example, from the larger category of criminal justice, Current Controversies deals with specific topics such as police brutality, gun control, white collar crime, and others. The debates in Current Controversies also are presented in a useful, timeless fashion. Articles and book excerpts included in each title are selected if they contribute valuable, long-range ideas to the overall debate. And wherever possible, current information is enhanced with historical documents and other relevant materials. Thus, while individual titles are current in focus, every effort is made to ensure that they will not become quickly outdated. Books in the Current Controversies series will remain important resources for librarians, teachers, and students for many years.

In addition to keeping the titles focused and specific, great care is taken in the editorial format of each book in the series.

Book introductions and chapter prefaces are offered to provide background material for readers. Chapters are organized around several key questions that are answered with diverse opinions representing all points on the political spectrum. Materials in each chapter include opinions in which authors clearly disagree as well as alternative opinions in which authors may agree on a broader issue but disagree on the possible solutions. In this way, the content of each volume in Current Controversies mirrors the mosaic of opinions encountered in society. Readers will quickly realize that there are many viable answers to these complex issues. By questioning each author's conclusions, students and casual readers can begin to develop the critical thinking skills so important to evaluating opinionated material.

Current Controversies is also ideal for controlled research. Each anthology in the series is composed of primary sources taken from a wide gamut of informational categories including periodicals, newspapers, books, United States and foreign government documents, and the publications of private and public organizations. Readers will find factual support for reports, debates, and research papers covering all areas of important issues. In addition, an annotated table of contents, an index, a book and periodical bibliography, and a list of organizations to contact are included in each book to expedite further research.

Perhaps more than ever before in history, people are confronted with diverse and contradictory information. During the Persian Gulf War, for example, the public was not only treated to minute-to-minute coverage of the war, it was also inundated with critiques of the coverage and countless analyses of the factors motivating U.S. involvement. Being able to sort through the plethora of opinions accompanying today's major issues, and to draw one's own conclusions, can be a complicated and frustrating struggle. It is the editors' hope that Current Controversies will help readers with this struggle.

Introduction

The cornerstone controversy in the overall debate concerning the elderly is whether society bears a responsibility for their well-being. Some believe that the elderly should be responsible for their own financial security and that families should care for their own members as they age. Others maintain that society should provide for the well-being of its elderly citizens through a public safety net of government benefits that provide health care, pension payments, and other support programs. One particular controversy within the overall debate over society's responsibility for the elderly is whether younger generations should subsidize the benefits of the aging population. Some contend that each generation should pay for its own benefits while others claim that the responsibility should be shared.

The U.S. Census Bureau expects that by 2050 more Americans will be over sixty than under eighteen. The 76 million people born between 1946 and 1964, known as the baby boom generation, is aging, and younger generations will be competing with baby boomers for resources. Some fear that retiring boomers will strain Medicare, the government's health insurance for seniors, and Social Security, the government's pension program. Anyone who contributes to Social Security during their working life can begin collecting benefits at age sixty-two, and all Americans over sixty-five qualify for Medicare, regardless of income. When people retire, however, they stop paying the payroll taxes that fund these programs. As a result, when the large population of baby boomers retires, the number of people who collect benefits from such programs will rise sharply while the number of workers who contribute will decline.

Those who believe that each generation should be responsible for itself, a value system known as generational autonomy or generational equity, contend that younger workers will bear an unfair burden if they are forced to pay for aging baby boomers. Demographers Jagadeesh Gokhale and Laurence Kotlikoff contend that the retirement of aging baby boomers "will mark the beginning of an enormous conflict over resources. Indeed, it is probably no exaggeration to say that we are approaching generational warfare." After funding public benefits for aging boomers, generational autonomists argue, younger generations will not have sufficient resources remaining for their own eventual needs. According to Chris Edwards and Tad DeHaven of the Cato Institute, a conservative think tank, "Budget costs for the elderly must be radically cut. If entitlements are not reformed, young families will be laboring under a huge tax burden and receiving very little in return." These analysts tout privatization—the transfer of responsibility for traditionally public social and health services to the private sector—as the solution. They claim, for example, that privatizing Social Security, letting workers invest part of their Social Security money in personal retirement accounts, will increase personal responsibility, bring higher profits, and create generational equity.

Those who claim that responsibility for elderly benefits should be shared contend that the war between the generations is a false conflict contrived to get young people to support policies such as privatization that reduce intergenerational responsibility. In contrast to generational autonomy, those who promote generational interdependence reason that programs created for the benefit of one generation are in the best interest of all generations because they benefit society as a whole. For example, spending money on education benefits young people who are in turn more likely to find work and pay taxes that fund programs that benefit the elderly. Health care spending on the elderly results in their living longer and the young in turn have the continued presence of older adults in their lives. In a 2005 speech U.S. senator Barack Obama

(D-Ill.) asked Americans, "After a lifetime of hard work and contribution to this country, do we tell our seniors that they're on their own, or that we're here for them to provide a basic standard of living? Is the dignity of life in their latter years their problem, or one we all share?" Obama asserts, "We're in this together—for our seniors, for our children, and for every American in the years and generations yet to come."

As baby boomers age over the next three decades, America will face major challenges as it reconciles the government's role in ensuring their well-being. The value system that emerges as dominant—generational autonomy or generational interdependence—will determine the course of public policy and spending on the elderly. The path ultimately chosen will have far-reaching implications for both today's seniors and the elderly in generations to come. The authors in *Current Controversies: The Elderly* represent a wide range of viewpoints in the debates concerning the growing elderly population and society's role in meeting its needs.

CHAPTER 1

Is the Growing Elderly Population a Serious Problem?

Chapter Preface

According to the U.S. Census Bureau, over the next three decades, the number of Americans age sixty-five and older is expected to grow to nearly 70 million—more than double the current population of Canada. Due to improved living conditions and modern medical care, people live longer today than they have at any other time in history. In 1900 life expectancy in the United States was just forty-seven years; today it is more than seventy-seven. The elderly are the fastest growing age group in the country.

The primary driving force behind this explosive growth is the aging of the baby boom generation—the 76 million people born between 1946 and 1964. The boomers are the nation's largest demographic group. The first members of this massive generation are nearing their sixties. By the year 2030, 20 percent of the population is estimated to be over sixty-five; in 2005 that figure is less than 13 percent.

Unlike the elderly of past generations, when death was primarily caused by accident or sudden illness, most elderly people now die from chronic conditions such as cancer, heart disease, or Alzheimer's. These conditions progress over time and require long-term medical care. More people today live for decades with ongoing health problems such as hypertension, arthritis, and diabetes, all of which can be medically managed. The number of people who will live into old age is therefore expected to increase dramatically. The number of those expected to live beyond eighty-five is projected to grow from 4.2 million in 1999 to 19 million by 2050. Few dispute that the growing elderly population will have a dramatic impact on social services, housing, and health care. The controversy centers on whether this impact—and the ways that society responds to it—will be positive or negative.

Many experts believe that the country is ill prepared to handle the influx of so many older adults at once. Gerontologist Ken Dychtwald coined the expression "age wave" to describe what he considers to be a looming crisis. Dychtwald and others are concerned that the elderly could bankrupt the nation as a growing number of seniors collect Social Security, Medicare, and other government benefits. They question whether enough trained caregivers will be available to care for the elderly. Moreover, they fear that the country's health care system will be overwhelmed and unable to care for so many people of advanced age, especially the millions expected to have Alzheimer's. Those who see population aging as a serious problem also point to a growing strain between the older and younger generations as they compete for scarce social and economic resources. They argue that planning, preparation, and policy reforms must begin now to avert certain catastrophe.

Other experts believe that doomsday predictions about population aging are exaggerated and that the demographic shift to a larger elderly population should be viewed as an opportunity, not a problem. Because aging baby boomers are healthier, wealthier, and more productive than past generations, many experts expect them to make significant contributions to society and to positively redefine what it means to be old in America. They emphasize that it is how society chooses to respond to the elderly that will either create problems or foster positive results.

Only time will tell whether the aging of the baby boom generation will be a blessing or a burden. The authors in the following chapter express their views in answer to the question, is the growing elderly population a serious problem?

The Growing Elderly Population Is a Serious Problem

Peter G. Peterson

Peter G. Peterson is senior chairman and cofounder of The Blackstone Group, a private investment banking firm, and a former chairman of the Federal Reserve Bank of New York.

The challenge of global aging, like a massive iceberg, looms ahead in the future of the largest and most affluent economies of the world. Visible above the waterline are the unprecedented growth in the number of elderly and the unprecedented decline in the number of youth over the next several decades. Lurking beneath the waves, and not yet widely understood, are the wrenching economic and social costs that will accompany this demographic transformation—costs that threaten to bankrupt even the greatest of powers, the United States included, unless they take action in time. Those who are most aware of the implications of this extraordinary demographic shift will best be able to prepare themselves for it, and even profit from the many opportunities it will leave in its wake.

A Long List of Hazards

The list of great hazards in the next century is long and generally familiar. It includes proliferation of nuclear, chemical, and biological weapons; high-tech terrorism; deadly superviruses; extreme climate change; the financial, economic, and political aftershocks of globalization; and the ethnic and military explosions waiting to be detonated by today's unsteady

new democracies. Yet there is a less-understood challenge—
the graying of the developed world's population—that may
actually do more to reshape our collective future than any of
the above.

This demographic shift cannot be avoided. It is inevitable.
The timing and magnitude of the coming transformation is
virtually locked in. The elderly of the first half of the next
century have already been born and can be counted—and the
retirement benefit systems on which they will depend are already in place. The future costs can therefore be projected
with a fair degree of certainty. Unlike global warming, for example, there can be little theoretical debate over whether global aging will manifest itself—or when. And unlike other challenges, such as financial support for new democracies, the cost
of global aging will be far beyond our means—even the collective means of all the world's wealthy nations. How we con-
front global aging will have direct economic implications—
measurable, over the next century, in the quadrillions of
dollars—that will likely dwarf the other challenges. Indeed, it
will greatly influence how the other challenges ultimately play
out.

---

*The challenge of global aging, like a massive iceberg,
looms ahead in the future of the largest and most affluent economies of the world.*

Societies in the developed world—by which I mean primarily the countries of North America, Western Europe, Japan, and Australia—are aging for three major reasons:

- Medical advances, along with increased affluence and
  improvement in public health, nutrition, and safety, are
  raising average life expectancy dramatically.

- A huge outsized baby boom generation in the United States and several other countries is now making its way through middle age.

- Fertility rates have fallen, and in Japan and a number of European countries are now running far beneath the "replacement rate" necessary to replace today's population. The impact of so few young people entering tomorrow's tax-paying workforce, while so many are entering benefit-receiving elderhood, is of profound consequence.

Global Aging Will Dominate the Agenda

As a result, I believe that global aging will become the transcendent political and economic issue of the twenty-first century. I will argue that—like it or not, and there's every reason to believe we won't like it—renegotiating the established social contract in response to global aging will soon dominate and daunt the public policy agendas of all the developed countries

---

The cost of global aging will be far beyond our means—even the collective means of all the world's wealthy nations.

By the 2030s, these countries will be much older than they are today. Some of them may exceed a median age of 55, twenty years older than the oldest median age (35) of *any* country on earth as recently as 1970. Over half of the adult population of today's developed countries and perhaps two-thirds of their voters will be near or beyond today's eligibility age for publicly financed retirement. So we have to ask: When that time comes, who will be doing the work, paying the taxes, saving for the future, and raising the next generation? Can even the wealthiest of nations afford to pay for such a vast number of senior citizens living a third or more of their adult lives in what are now commonly thought of as the retirement years? Or will many of those future elderly have to do without the retirement benefits they are now promised? And what happens then? . . .

Imposing as the challenge of an aging society is in the United States, it is even more serious in Japan and much of Europe. In most of the other developed countries, populations are aging faster, birthrates are lower, the influx of younger immigrants from developing countries is smaller, public pension benefits for senior citizens are more generous, and private pension systems are weaker. Most of the other leading economies therefore face far worse fiscal fundamentals than we do. Even some major developing countries—China, for example—face serious aging challenges in the next century.

Given the instant and sometimes painful interactions within global capital markets and the likelihood of varying national responses to the coming fiscal challenge, I can easily envision that sometime in the next decade or two demographic aging will trigger unprecedented financial pressures, both on fragile regional economic arrangements such as the European Economic and Monetary Union and on the world economy as a whole. The economic and political outcome could make today's Asian or Russian crisis look like child's play.

Demographic aging is, at bottom, a global challenge that cries out for a global solution. . . .

A Gray Dawn

A gray dawn is fast approaching. The more we know about this historic demographic transformation, the better prepared we will be. . . .

- *Global aging will transform the world into societies that are much older than any we have ever known or imagined.* Until the industrial revolution, the odds of encountering an elderly person (aged 65 or older) in an affluent nation was about 1 in 40. By 1990 it was about 1 in 10. In a few decades, it will be 1 in 4—and in the fastest-aging countries, 1 in 3 or even higher. By 2015, most developed countries will have more elders as a share of their population than the state of Florida has today.

- *As the number of elderly explodes, global aging will place an unprecedented economic burden on working-age people.* Today the ratio of working taxpayers to nonworking pensioners in the developed world is around 3 to 1. By 2030, absent reform, this ratio will fall to 1.5 to 1—and in some countries, such as Germany and Italy, it will drop all the way down to 1 to 1 or even lower. Thus, in the year 2030, the typical working couple will be required to fund the full cash pension and health-care needs of at least one anonymous retiree.

- *Global aging is what happens when people start living much longer.* Global life expectancies have grown more over the last fifty years than over the previous five thousand. Perhaps two-thirds of all the people who have ever lived to the age of 65 are alive today. Over the next thirty years, global life expectancy is projected to rise by another seven or eight years. This advance alone will raise the number of elderly by roughly one-third.

- *Even among the elderly, the number of "old old" (aged 85 and over) is growing much faster than the number of "young old"—a phenomenon demographers call "the aging of the aged."* Over the next fifty years, while the number of people aged 65 to 84 is projected to triple, the number of those aged 85 and over is projected to grow sixfold. In the United States, these old old consume twice as much hospital care per capita— and over twenty times as much nursing-home care—as elders between ages 65 and 74.

- *Global aging is also what happens when people start having fewer babies.* Thirty years ago, the typical woman worldwide had 5.0 children over her lifetime. Today that figure is 2.7. Meanwhile, the "total fertility rate" in the developed countries has fallen all the way to 1.6—which is already 25 percent beneath the rate necessary to replace the population generation to generation.

- *Global aging is pushing the developed world—and perhaps even the entire world—toward eventual population decline.* By the 2020s, working-age populations will be declining in virtually every developed country. By the year 2050, all the developed countries will likely shrink from 15 to 10 percent of the world population—while the Mideast, Central Asia, Africa, and Latin America will climb from 48 to 60 percent. Absent sizable immigration—and unless their fertility rates rise again— Western Europe and Japan will shrink to about one-half of their current population before the end of the twenty-first century.

- *Global aging will revolutionize the family, by drastically narrowing and lengthening its shape.* While the family tree narrows—and the number of a typical person's siblings, cousins, and children enters a steep decline—the surge in life expectancy will make the tree taller. Early in the next century, many developed countries will have more grandparents than grandchildren.

- *The official projections may err on the side of optimism, since they assume that the underlying causes of global aging will weaken over time.* In the United States, for example, life expectancy is officially forecast to rise no higher by the year 2050 than it already is in Japan today. Yet some experts believe that scientific advances will greatly increase longevity—even to 100 years or more. As for fertility, most official forecasts assume that women will have as many or more children in the future—not fewer—than they are having today.

Unprecedented Questions

In an aging world, every sphere of social life will experience profound changes and grapple with unprecedented questions. . . .

- *In economics and business:* As populations shrink, will economies shrink as well? What business sectors will be most affected? Does aging mean declining savings and sluggish productivity? Will the exploding cost of retirement benefits trigger massive budget deficits and overwhelm global capital markets? With what negative effects?

- *In ethics:* What happens as medical progress inevitably confronts increasingly scarce public resources? How will we decide whether to spend an extra dollar on the latest high-tech treatment for the old or on education and training for the young? How will all this reshape the ethics of life and death? Who lives? Who dies? Who decides?

- *In politics:* As the number of elderly swells, will the senior benefit lobbies become ever-more powerful and lay claim to an ever-larger share of public budgets? Will young people remain apathetic, even in the face of the unthinkable tax bills they will soon be paying? Or does generational war loom?

- *In culture:* How will global aging change people's outlook on life? Think of marketing. For many decades, the most targeted "demographic" among advertisers and media executives was the 18- to 49-year-old age group. That's because it was big, and its members spent. But already today, the most densely populated age bracket is getting older—and so the targeted demographic is getting older with it. What's sold to them, and how it's sold, is changing and will continue to change. What will TV be like when the median viewer is aged 40? And what will automobiles be like when the median driver is aged 50? What about Hollywood? Or Broadway? Or Madison Avenue? How will aging affect society's power to innovate and to imagine and create a new future?

- *In world affairs:* In an increasingly volatile world, will metastasizing public retirement spending choke off resources available for vital defense and multinational priorities? With youth so scarce, will sending large combat forces in harm's way become politically unacceptable? If older developed countries try to depend on the savings of younger developing countries, how will this change the global balance of power?

Graying Means Paying

I do not subscribe to a lugubrious view of demographic aging. In many respects, population aging is a highly positive transformation, a triumph of modern science. A great number of today's elders are energetic and talented, with serious contributions to make. They can teach younger people the wisdom that comes only from experience. They can provide leadership and guidance—comfort, too. This potential is eloquently described in a number of recent books, most notably President Jimmy Carter's *Virtues of Aging*. It's good that more grandchildren will know, really know, their grandparents and great-grandparents. (Perhaps this will help heal the strains the nuclear family has undergone in recent years.) There may be less crime as the population ages, since crime, especially violent crime, is a young man's game. The old are often more religious than the young, and here too they have much to teach.

So there is much good that can come from longer lifespans. But along with the good is the inescapable fact that graying means paying—paying for pensions, for hospitals, for doctors and nurses, for nursing homes and related social services.

Global aging will become the transcendent political and economic issue of the twenty-first century.

[By 2030], the official projections suggest that governments in most developed countries will have to spend at least an extra 9 to 16 percent of GDP [gross domestic product] annually simply to meet their old-age benefit promises. To pay these costs through increased taxation would raise the total tax burden by an unthinkable extra 25 to 40 percent of every worker's taxable wages—in countries where total payroll tax rates often already exceed 40 percent. Or, if we resort to deficit spending, we would have to consume all the savings and more of the entire developed world.

For the developed countries, the unfunded liabilities for pensions alone are about $35 trillion. Including healthcare, the figure is at least twice as much. To paraphrase the old quiz show, this makes the global issue at least a "$64 trillion question." Should we continue to ignore this problem, personal living standards will stagnate or decline and all other public spending priorities—whether basic research or the environment or education or defense—will be crowded out of public budgets. Our economies, our governments, and our democracies may find it hard to bear this enormous pressure. Furthermore, the official projections may be a best-case scenario, since they ignore the negative feedback effects of the mounting fiscal burden on the economy—through more borrowing, higher interest rates, more taxes, less savings, and lower rates of productivity and wage growth.

If we don't prepare for this challenge, much of what is good about an aging society could turn sour. After all, how will young and old live happily together if they see themselves as competitors for scarce resources? And, if this comes to pass, what wisdom will the old have after all to offer the young? And who among the young will listen? I very much respect the gifts that aging individuals can give to our communities and culture: But will the aged be praised for increasing the quality of life if they are deemed responsible for bankrupting the global economy?

The Growing Elderly Population Will Create a Health Care Worker Shortage

Kim Krisberg

Kim Krisberg writes about public health issues for Nation's Health, *the official newspaper of the American Public Health Association.*

While preparedness is a fundamental component of public health—from bioterrorism readiness to immunizations to disaster relief—some advocates say there is one major issue for which the health work force is woefully underprepared: the aging of America.

In 25 years, about one-fifth of all Americans will be ages 65 or older and, presumably, all will need a variety of health care services. In fact, older adults use more health care services than any other age group, making up half of physicians' visits and half of all hospital stays, according to the Centers for Disease Control and Prevention [CDC]. Not only will the demand for health services begin to overwhelm the supply in coming decades, health care spending is also expected to soar as more people become eligible for Medicare and Medicaid and depend more heavily on their private insurance providers.

But even though demand is expected to rise, few public health professionals are choosing to meet the challenge. A 2004 CDC report on the "State of Aging and Health in America" found that out of 650,000 practicing physicians in the United States, fewer than 9,000 are geriatricians and that number is expected to drop to 6,000 in coming years. On the education front, "geriatricians comprise only one-half of 1 percent of all medical educators in the (United States), which represents the largest education training gap in any field," the report stated. In addition to knowledge gaps, experts are also predicting shortages among workers such as home health and nursing home aides even as the demand for long-term care increases. For example, according to the National Governors Association, "by 2025, Texas alone will need over 55,000 additional paraprofessional health care aides to maintain current levels of care."

Although chronic disease prevention and health promotion will be key to sustaining quality of life in later years, advocates worry that a serious dearth in geriatric knowledge among health professionals will limit the number of positive outcomes. For example, it's well-known that regular physical exercise can delay or prevent the onset of chronic disease, increase independence and confidence and provides mental health benefits. However, because older people are underrepresented in many clinical trials and research programs, relatively little is known about what motivates older people to exercise, what keeps them exercising regularly and what exercise methods are best for those with certain conditions, such as arthritis.

Few Students Pursue Aging Careers

"In schools of public health, in medical schools and nursing schools, people don't learn enough about how to care for the aging population," said APHA member Nancy Alfred Persily, MPH, associate dean at the University of Albany School of Public Health. "(Public health) focused on (maternal and child health) for a long time, but we didn't think about what we need to really prevent more disability in aging populations. We're not educating people to look at aging as a special area that we need in public health."

According to Persily, taking on the work force shortage will require education and government efforts, from infusing aging issues into curriculums to examining how Medicare reimbursement rates affect worker recruitment and retention. She also said the long-term care field lacks strong leaders.

"We have leaders that look academically at the scientific part of aging ... but we don't have that cadre of people who really have been educated in management, strategic planning and elder care to be able to lead the country, lead organizations and sit at the table with the other people in health care to focus on what we can do for the aging," Persily told the *Nation's Health.*

About 2,800 additional medical school graduates will be needed annually to meet predicted demand [for geriatric care].

The coming boom in older Americans, Persily added, is compounded even more by predictions that many health professionals will be retiring at about the same time the demand for health care services is rising. According to the U.S. Health Resources and Services Administration [HRSA], the ability to attract more workers to the aging field to replace retirees is questionable, as the proportion of people ages 18 to 30 is declining. With the exception of a few states, most don't seem to be addressing health care work force shortages or retention problems, HRSA has reported, and many that are addressing the problems are only doing so with "modest" efforts. However, a number of non-profit organizations have stepped up to the plate.

"We really need to be looking at 2015 and beyond because it takes at least 10 years to produce a physician," said Edward Salsberg, MPA, director of the Center for Workforce Studies at the Association of American Medical Colleges. "Currently, I do not think we're adequately prepared, both in terms of the number and the skill sets."

The Center for Workforce Studies was created [in 2004] to collect data and conduct studies around the supply and demand of physicians and to advise the training community about the future need for physicians, Salsberg said. And the need to train more physicians isn't only directed toward geriatricians—"the reality is that for almost all specialties . . . a large percent of their patients are over 65, so we're going to need all sorts of more physicians," he noted. According to the center, about 2,800 additional medical school graduates will be needed annually to meet predicted demand, although Salsberg predicted "we're going to need a lot more than that."

Training Is a Core Issue

Graduating more physicians with knowledge of aging issues is a multi-faceted problem that will require creative solutions. Although there has been work to increase geriatric curriculums in medical schools, the demands on medical students are so high given the always increasing body of knowledge, that the challenge is finding the time for additional education. In turn, the solution is not to simply add on aging curriculum, but to "infuse the current curriculum with more information and skills around the needs of the elderly," Salsberg told the *Nation's Health*.

"The issue of curriculum reform is really across the spectrum of all medical education and training and I think we're still assessing our understanding of the best role for geriatricians," he said.

The health care system isn't designed well for geriatricians, Salsberg noted. For example, people build relationships with their health care providers over many years and are unlikely to switch their primary care to a geriatrician simply because they've grown older. The question arises, Salsberg said, whether it is better to have a geriatrician take over a person's lead care or to use geriatricians as consultants. Of course, one of the best ways to prepare for an aging America and limit the impact of a work force shortage is to step up prevention, he said.

"I think the wisest investment would probably be in prevention," Salsberg said. "It strikes me as foolish to just focus on needing more doctors and not simultaneously say 'let's do what we can to keep the elderly healthy.'"

Unfortunately, there's relatively little investment at national agencies, such as CDC, in aging issues and for the average public health department, such health concerns aren't "really on the radar screen," according to Robyn Stone, DrPH, executive director of the Institute for the Future of Aging Services at the American Association of Homes and Services for the Aging.

"I think we are a very much aging-adverse society and it plays out in our health care systems," Stone told the *Nation's Health*.

Stone said the work force gap begins with "pervasive ageism" in the United States—that our fear of growing old, or even talking about growing old, has affected how society values those who care for the elderly.

"Our society really doesn't value those jobs, so there's not the same monetary value attached to (them)," she said. There are two major issues, according to Stone: shortages and preparation of quality professionals. While much of the labor shortage for front-line caregivers is determined by competition in local economies, the "ongoing problem of preparing and retaining a quality work force is the more fundamental problem," she said. Stone predicted that the nation has about a 20-year window to prepare itself to meet the demands of older residents.

"We've got to shift the paradigm of teaching to understand that our primary client will be the elderly," Stone said.

To help prepare the nation, the Institute for the Future of Aging Services runs the Better Jobs Better Care program, a four-year, multi-million dollar research and demonstration program funded by the Robert Wood Johnson Foundation and Atlantic Philanthropies. The program aims to create changes in long-term care policy and workplace practices, among other goals, said Debra Lipson, MHSA, deputy director of Better Jobs Better Care. In the arena of long-term care, not only do many workers not have the proper training, but the pool of workers who traditionally filled such jobs is decreasing. According to Lipson, the long-term care work force has traditionally consisted of middle-aged women with little education, but that population is shrinking as more women go on to higher education and fewer women are available to stay at home as caregivers for elderly relatives.

Wages in the Field Are Low

Also, the average wage for a nursing home aide is about $8.90 per hour, often with health benefits, while the average for a home care worker is only about $7.80, even though most people want to be taken care of in their homes, Lipson said. Adding to problems is the fact that about two-thirds of all nursing home residents have their bills paid for by state Medicaid programs, and with health care costs busting state budgets, state legislators do their best to keep pay rates low.

"You get what you pay for, and in this case, (some states) are buying services on the cheap," Lipson told the *Nation's Health*. "There will ultimately have to be some sort of publicly subsidized insurance program or something else that provides real protection from the catastrophic cost of long-term care so that it doesn't fall on the states."

To increase the quality of long-term care, Better Jobs Better Care awarded grants to five demonstration projects in 2003 to projects in Vermont, Pennsylvania, North Carolina, Iowa and Oregon. For example, in North Carolina, the grantee is setting up a process through which long-term care employers can apply for special licensures after having met standards for areas such as supervisory practices and safe workloads. Ideally, such employers will be able to use the licensures in their efforts to recruit more qualified workers and as part of their client marketing campaigns. In turn, a better prepared and more knowledgeable work force will hopefully result in better wages and benefits and higher retention rates, according to Lipson.

We're hitting a crisis situation among public health professionals who have special expertise in healthy aging.

Another project at Better Jobs Better Care is looking at how to recruit non-traditional labor pools such as people ages 55 to 65 as well as those who have experience caring for an elderly family member.

"(Such workers) are not health professionals by definition and yet they are critical to the quality of care for people who need long-term care," Lipson said.

However, before people reach the stage of long-term care, there are many opportunities for health promotion and the delay of chronic disease and disability that are missed, said APHA member Fox Wetle, PhD, associate dean of Medicine for Public Health and Public Policy at Brown University. The research into how to change older people's health behavior is minimal, and when effective methods are found, oftentimes there isn't enough funding to implement them, Wetle said.

"We're hitting a crisis situation among public health professionals who have special expertise in healthy aging," she told the *Nation's Health.*

To begin reversing the work force trend, health curriculums must begin adjusting and national investments must be made to encourage students to study aging, she said.

"It's very important that these investments be made," Wetle said. "We either make the investment now or we pay big-time later."

Aging Prisoners Strain the Nation's Penal System

Stephanie Pfeffer

Stephanie Pfeffer writes for Medill News Service, a news wire service staffed by graduate journalism students at Northwestern University.

A 70-year-old man takes his daily dose of Alzheimer's medication. A 54-year-old cancer patient faints after not eating for two days. A 67-year-old stroke victim sits motionless, confined to his wheelchair.

Sound like a hospital? A nursing home?

It's actually a common scenario in state and federal prisons, where an estimated 125,000 people over age 50 are currently incarcerated, according to Richard Aday, author of the book *Aging Prisoners: Crisis in American Corrections....*

[An infrequently] talked about issue is the implications three-strikes laws and harsh sentences have on an already burdened prison system by crowding it with aging prisoners.

"It's definitely a crisis," said Aday. "It's the graying of the prison population."

According to a report by The Sentencing Project, a nonprofit group that promotes decreased reliance on incarceration, if California continues to admit 1,200 three-strikes felons annually, by the year 2026 there will be approximately 30,000 inmates serving sentences of 25 years to life in the state, at a conservative cost of $750 million a year.

"Overcrowding is not upfront. It's in the long run," said Ryan King, one of the report's authors. "The real rise in prison population is from people coming in and not coming out."

The Number of Elderly Prisoners Is Growing

Under three-strikes laws, older men are being given longer sentences. This is because admitted third strikers, who are punished most severely, already have a lengthy criminal record. They're older than the average admitted prisoner. In California, for example, the average age of a sentenced third striker is about 36, while the average age of non–third strikers is 34, according to The Sentencing Project report. Nationally, the average age of admitted non–third strikers is about 31.

While three-strikes legislation contributes to the aging prison population, it's not the only culprit. Other harsh sentencing policies such as mandatory minimums and truth in sentencing are also leaving criminals in prison longer. "The elderly and other people have gotten caught up in these sentencing laws," according to Aday.

There are approximately 125,000 elderly prisoners nationwide, about 11 percent of the total prison population.

"The judges' hands are tied," he continued, explaining that mandatory sentences strip judges of their discretion to provide clemency or shorten sentences based on circumstances of the case. This is coupled with a reduced reliance on parole; some states have completely disbanded their parole boards. "It takes away from incentives for inmates to get an education or go through counseling to be eligible for parole," Aday noted.

Other reasons for the increase in aging prisoners are the aging of the general population, which is reflected in prisons, and the boom in prison construction of the 1990s, which left many beds waiting to be filled.

Just how many aging prisoners are there? Using 50 as the defining age, there are approximately 125,000 elderly prisoners nationwide, about 11 percent of the total prison population.

California's three-strikes law has directly contributed to the aging prison population since its 1994 inception. The number of people admitted for felonies over the age of 40 increased from about 15 percent in 1994 to 23 percent by 1999, according to data from the California Department of Corrections. This contrasts with the general decline in prison admissions for all age groups between 20 and 35.

The Life of an Elderly Inmate

There are three types of aging inmates, Aday explained. There are "lifers," who have been in prison for their whole lives, new elderly offenders, who are sentenced in their 40s or 50s, and chronic re-offenders, who have been in and out of prison consistently.

For all types, prison conditions can be very stressful.

"If you are 70 years old and you just came into prison, you are isolated for the first time from family," Aday said. "It's hard experiencing all those types of losses simultaneously."

Studies show that elderly prisoners need more orderly conditions, safety precautions, emotional feedback and familial support than younger prisoners. They are especially uncomfortable in crowded conditions and tend to want time alone.

The relationship between older and younger inmates is also problematic. According to Aday, most elderly prisoners are still integrated with other age groups, leaving them susceptible to intimidation and thievery. "[Older inmates] are very vulnerable to the population that's stronger than them," Aday said.

"The fear of becoming a victim can have an impact on their daily life," he continued. For example, one Texas facility houses aging prisoners in separate cells from younger inmates but forces everyone to mix in the yard. Many older inmates are so scared of mingling that they don't go outside.

There are also numerous medical concerns facing elderly prisoners, such as the lack of an adequate or balanced diet and insufficient preventive health care.

From a health standpoint, elderly prisoners are about 10 years older than their chronological age due to characteristics of their lives before entering prison. Low socioeconomic status, lack of access to health care, drug or alcohol use and years of living a hard life have taken their toll.

Nationally, the typical inmate costs $20–$25,000 [a year]. Frail, elderly inmates can cost three times as much to incarcerate, about $60–65,000 a year.

According to the *Sourcebook of Criminal Justice Statistics*, more than 47 percent of state prisoners over age 45 reported a physical impairment or mental condition in 1997, compared with about 30 percent of prisoners of all ages.

A medical source at the Richard J. Donovan Correctional Facility in San Diego said the most common illnesses among elderly men in prison are diabetes and hepatitis C. Many are on dialysis machines, receive oxygen or have cancer.

"Some of these guys are very sick," he said. Diabetes is especially problematic because non-medical prisons rarely cater to those with special dietary needs. Prisoners with diabetes usually eat the same food as other inmates, meals full of sugar and carbohydrates. "A pancake loaded with syrup," is a common breakfast, he said.

Female prisoners are at an even greater health risk. At just two percent of the prison population, their needs are most neglected. "Older females, oftentimes grandmothers, have special health care needs that are very distinct from men," Aday said. Necessary health programs like therapeutic services, cervical and breast cancer screenings and nutritional meals containing calcium and fresh vegetables are not widely available.

Medical Costs Are High

Health care is the second largest expense facing prisons, after security. The annual cost for housing a typical prisoner in California is about $26,000, according to the California Department of Corrections. Nationally, the typical inmate costs $20–25,000. Frail, elderly inmates can cost three times as much to incarcerate, about $60–65,000 a year.

At Kentucky State Reformatory, even though one fatally ill inmate wanted his life to end, "the prison cannot permit him to not receive health care," Aday said. His care was outsourced to a hospital; the total cost before death was $500,000.

The Sentencing Project estimates that in California, an elderly prisoner incarcerated for a minimum of 25 years can cost $1.5 million.

"It's always important to make our streets safe and there are some people who should be in prison, but at what cost?" Aday asked.

"Given that the average third-strike inmate enters prison at the age of 36, he or she will have a minimum of 21 years left in prison after the age of 39," King wrote in the Sentencing Project report. This means that 60-year-olds, and even 70-year-olds, are still serving time.

However, only one percent of all serious crimes are committed by people over age 60, according to the American Civil Liberties Union. Indeed, criminologists have long known that most crimes are committed by people in their late teens and early 20s. In California, for example, only 22 percent of all felony adult arrests in 1999 were people over age 39, reports the Sentencing Project. Only 5 percent were above 50 years old.

"People just age out of crime," said King. It's why three-strikes "doesn't make good sense" from a policy perspective, he said.

There are several types of solutions to combat an at-risk, rapidly aging prison population.

The most immediate step is to increase preventive care and educate prisoners to eat better, exercise and monitor their own health. It's important that they receive the necessary medical treatment, whether it be special meals or proper cancer screenings, Aday said.

Another practical option is building long-term care facilities for aging inmates, like nursing homes or in-prison hospices. Other alternatives include halfway houses or house arrest, both more appropriate for a non-violent elderly offender than a maximum-security prison.

In the long run, the only way to stop the rapid influx of aging inmates is to reinstate the softer sentencing laws and give more power back to judges. This is already beginning to happen, according to King. "There's been a shift in the last couple of years and states have begun to reconsider," he said. "They are starting to roll back."

"The political climate is acceptable for discussing alternatives," he concluded.

Doomsday Predictions About Population Aging Are Exaggerated

Robert B. Friedland and Laura Summer

Robert Friedland and Laura Summer are the authors of "Demography Is Not Destiny, Revisited," a 1999 report that refuted alarmist views about population aging. Friedland is the founding director of the Georgetown University Center on an Aging Society, which studies the impact of demographic changes on public and private institutions and families. Summer is deputy director of the center and is a senior researcher at the university's Health Policy Institute.

That our society is aging is well known. Media stories and political rhetoric abound concerning the impending demographic challenges as the population age 65 and older is anticipated to more than double by the year 2030. Much of the handwringing concerns an expectation of dire fiscal consequences for publicly financed programs, such as Medicare and Social Security, of which older people tend to be the principal beneficiaries.

What is not said is that planning for the future on the basis of demographic projections alone is a fool's game. Population projections can be wrong, but even if they turn out to be correct, other factors, particularly those related to the economy and public policies, can have a decidedly greater impact on the future than simply the growing number and proportion of older people. What is needed for wise policy planning is a close look at the range of influences on our future and the willingness to make choices to use some of our wealth to invest in the future.

Robert B. Friedland and Laura Summer, "Demography Is Not Destiny, Revisited," Center on Aging Society, Georgetown University, March 2005. Copyright © 2005 by The Commonwealth Fund. Reproduced by permission.

No doubt the future will be different from the past. Yet we can take solace by looking to the past. After all, some of the anticipated demographic changes, like the doubling of the population age 65 and older, have already occurred. The population is anticipated to grow older than it is now, but the population is already older now than it has ever been. Moreover, demographically the United States is considerably younger than most other industrialized countries. What can we learn by looking to the past and understanding how the economy and public policies interacted with demographic changes? And what can we learn by looking at older nations as well?

This report provides a framework and some of the basic data necessary to understand why our future is not determined solely by the anticipated changes in the size and age distribution of the population. Themes repeated throughout this report include:

- Demography is not destiny. The choices made through the political process and through market forces, in conjunction with demographic changes, will determine the future.

- The critical challenge of an aging society is not so much how to accommodate the older population, but how to ensure the productivity of future workers, regardless of age.

- In the future, older persons are likely to be at least as diverse in terms of their health, financial status, and ethnic origins as their predecessors. Not all racial and ethnic populations have benefited from past economic growth to the same extent. Some groups are extremely vulnerable.

- Uncovered health and long-term care expenses leave everyone fiscally vulnerable, but particularly affect older persons.

- Public policies that encourage and facilitate education, basic research, and the application of promising technologies can enhance the well-being of current and future generations of older people.

- Greater economic growth can make policy choices easier, but deciding how much of the proceeds of economic growth to use collectively and how to distribute costs and benefits will require political and policy choices.

Future demographic change is much easier to anticipate than other forms of change. At any point in the past century, one could have easily anticipated a dramatic increase in the size and proportion of the population age 65 and older. Since 1900, the number of Americans age 65 and older has doubled three times. Since 1960, the population age 65 and older has doubled while the overall population has only grown 57 percent. However, since 1960 the nation's income (as measured by real gross domestic product) has nearly quadrupled.

Economic Growth Matters

Economic growth has made the nation more prosperous and has enabled many to enjoy a higher standard of living than would have been possible a generation earlier. Although income and wealth are not distributed equally, most families have seen their material standard of living improve with each generation.

Many wonder if the country can support an aging society. Most of this anxiety is directed at one aspect of aging: federal entitlement spending. In 1998, the Commission on Retirement Policy predicted "rapid increases in entitlement spending ... spiraling deficits ... huge revenue needs ... a burden on future generations." In 1995, the Bipartisan Commission on Entitlement and Tax Reform warned that "... the projected imbalance between spending and revenues—particularly with regard to health care and retirement entitlement programs—

will, together with interest on the federal debt, undermine America's capacity to make appropriate investments in the well being of our citizens and undertake other essential government functions, such as national defense."

There are legitimate reasons to be concerned about growth in expenditures, but there is more reason to be concerned about economic growth. With little economic growth society faces fewer choices on how to care for those who are least able to care for themselves. With sufficient economic growth there are more choices and fewer persons in need. Small differences in sustained economic growth will have a dramatic impact on the fiscal future of society. If real economic growth averages about 2 percent per year between now and 2050, then, depending on the policy choices we make, government expenditures as a proportion of the economy in 2050 might not be substantially larger than today and we will still be able to meet the promises made to future beneficiaries.

The population age 65 to 75 is healthier, wealthier, and better educated than . . . past generations.

It would be foolish to assume society will simply grow its way out of the difficult choices that the aging of the population will require. It would be equally foolish to assume that the future will be completely dismal if there is no radical restructuring of government programs. If public policies support the market transitions necessary for economic growth during demographic transitions, then we can afford to meet the challenges of the retirement of the baby boom.

Tomorrow's Seniors Will Be Different

Life today is different from the past, in part because of demographic and economic changes. The population age 65 to 75 is healthier, wealthier, and better educated than persons in this age group in past generations. Future groups of older people are likely to be even better off. They too will redefine "retirement" and "old age."

Older persons still remain vulnerable Improvements across age groups should not blind us to the fact that certain segments of the population age 65 and older remain very vulnerable. Older single women, for example, have particularly low average incomes. There is also substantial variation in the educational attainment of baby boomers. Because people with more education tend to have higher incomes and better health, this educational disparity virtually guarantees a diverse group of older people in the future. Current financial disparities are expected to persist or grow. And large health and long-term care expenses can substantially drain the resources of even those who previously felt financially secure.

Insuring risks Social insurance—in the form of Social Security, disability insurance, unemployment insurance, and Medicare—is designed to improve the economic security of workers and their dependents. These programs, along with private insurance and tax incentives for individual savings and employee benefits, have pooled financial risk and contributed to the well-being of American families. However, longer life expectancy has accentuated the financial risks of health and long-term care by highlighting increasingly large gaps in public programs and private insurance. Some of the gaps in coverage are filled by public assistance, such as Medicaid and Supplemental Security Income. However, many gaps are not filled, resulting in homelessness, hunger, and higher proportions of unmet and uncompensated health care needs.

Policy Matters

Population growth and change will affect society, but so too will policy choices. Much of the concern over the anticipated growth in the older population is related to anxiety about the federal budget. The budget issues may be significant, but the federal budget is just one facet of the economy. Policymakers must not only evaluate the tax-financed expenditures of programs like Medicare and Social Security, they must also consider the net impact these expenditures have and changes that would occur if these programs did not exist.

With reasonable economic growth, projected government spending will not be substantially larger as a percentage of national income than it is today. With less economic growth, tougher choices—related to cutting program benefits or raising taxes—will have to be made. But given the likelihood of some economic growth, the debate about future government spending is likely to be a debate mostly about how to distribute the additional wealth in the economy.

Issues related to the aging of our society pale in comparison to the ... challenges our society has already faced.

Currently, much of the public discussion about an aging society involves how to finance Social Security and Medicare. Resolving this question will have an impact on financial security for future age groups but will do little to resolve the implications for communities. Reducing the share of public support does not eliminate societal costs, it merely leaves individuals and their families responsible for a larger share, and some of those costs end up getting shifted back to the public sector through less direct and often more expensive means. Families and local communities will face a wide array of issues related to education, housing, social services, and transportation that will not be answered by cutting, expanding, or restructuring entitlement programs.

The Future Will Bring Challenges

Issues related to the aging of our society pale in comparison to the social, political, military, and economic challenges our society has already faced. With little planning, society has adjusted to the baby boom and to the consequences of large numbers of people moving through the schools, the labor force, and the housing, product, and financial markets.

The baby boom is now anticipated to begin moving out of the labor force and into the realm of health care, long-term care, and claims on retirement income. Society can and will adjust. But the transitions and their consequences will be easier the better prepared we are. As policymakers decide on policies to meet this challenge, they must recognize that those policies will have to change as everything else changes. This suggests maintaining flexibility to allow such changes to be made as the future becomes clearer.

The Growing Elderly Population Is Healthier and Wealthier than Ever

Tim Smart

Tim Smart writes about personal finance and business for U.S. News and World Report, *a weekly newsmagazine.*

Madonna Bron, 52, who has clocked more than 50 marathons since a heart attack at 37, is often up before dawn for a daily run. Ron Cohen, 55, left the corporate rat race eight years ago, "downsized" from an executive job in Boston, for the laid-back air of western North Carolina—now he manages 15 people and runs an 11-vehicle transportation service. And Carol Kraker, 51, rises early most mornings for a swim before starting her 10-to-12-hour day selling upscale retirement homes outside Phoenix.

You call this retirement? Forget quiet lolls in a porch rocking chair, with morning golf followed by afternoon naps and "early bird" suppers. The first of the 78-million-strong baby boom generation turn 55 this year [2001]. And just as they changed life as we know it in recent decades—from music to marriage to mutual funds—this healthy, wealthy, and wise band of "zoomers" is charging toward retirement at its own breakneck speed.

Much as they transformed the suburbs, bringing forth the "soccer mom" phenomenon, demographers anticipate the boomer generation will rewrite what it means to be a senior citizen. They'll take tai chi classes in their 90s, start second careers at 60, and begin romances at ages that will bring frowns to the foreheads of their grandkids.

Healthy and Wealthy

They will be a force to reckon with. Boomers make up almost a third of the U.S. population, and they are aging fast. Beginning in 2000, boomers started turning 50 at the rate of just under 10,000 a day. Already, more than 14 million boomers are 50 and up, and some aren't waiting until 55 to take early retirement. It's a well-educated crowd: Nearly 90 percent of boomers graduated from high school, and more than a quarter have at least a bachelor's degree. More than three quarters own homes, and 73 percent have some form of investments. And the eldest among them have money: A recent AARP [American Association of Retired Persons] report on the 50-plus generation shows those in the top quartile [fourth] had a median income of $100,000 and a median net worth of $360,000.

Boomers are generally far better equipped for retirement than their parents were.

But the bounty is not evenly distributed. Those in the bottom fourth had a median income of just $10,000 and were disproportionately female. "The top quarter are way ahead of where their parents were" heading into retirement, says AARP's director of legislation and public policy, John Rother. "The middle half is somewhat better off. The bottom quarter is in trouble; their wages have not kept up with the economy." The stock market slump hasn't helped, nor the double-digit annual increases in healthcare costs. For the first time in many years, [the 2001] Retirement Confidence Survey found a drop in the percentage of workers saving for retirement (from 75 percent in 2000 to 71 percent [in 2001]) and a dip in confidence about meeting retirement income goals.

The income disparity highlights a signal fact about the boomers—their diversity. Despite attempts by marketers and the media to brand them as one, perhaps the most common trait of the generation born between 1946 and 1964 is its individuality. "The boomers have been a very distinct generation all the way," says Milken Institute demographer William Frey. "They have broken the mold in every conceivable way. I can't imagine them really changing as they age."

Certainly not if Kraker is the mold. At 47, she and husband Randy bought a home at Sun City Grand, an active-adult community (retirement is no longer a word used by those who market to the 55-plus crowd) near Phoenix close to the original Sun City retirement community where her in-laws live. "I really did fight it, actually," she says about leaving her job as a human-resources manager for a Minnesota casino. "All the way down here, I was on the cellphone talking to the casino." After six months without work, Kraker took a job snapping pictures of high school kids while earning her real-estate license. Now, she's one of the top producers in her firm. Her husband, meanwhile, downshifted from an executive's job to that of a salesman for the industrial chemicals firm he worked for in Minnesota. For fun, she sky-dives; both are in a local theater group. "I can't believe how much stress is gone," she says of her new life.

Dual Incomes

Retirement experts say Kraker is emblematic of the zoomer generation: independent, youthful, with prospects of a long life ahead, and well off. Their bank accounts fattened with years of appreciation in their primary homes and their company-sponsored retirement accounts, their bodies strengthened by years of exercise, their minds stimulated by college and sometimes postgraduate educations, boomers are generally far better equipped for retirement than their parents were. Many will be in households where there is not just one, but two earners, with multiple retirement savings accounts gathered over the years at different jobs.

Forever Young?

It is also the realization that even if they work in retirement, as 80 percent of those in a 1998 AARP survey said they think they will, life without the all-defining career might be less than fulfilling to boomers. "We're never short of things to do," says Hegreness. But, he adds, "there's a certain guilt feeling we harbor. We're not really contributing to society." After all, this is the generation whose anthem included the memorable lyric of the Who's "My Generation": "Hope I die before I get old."

That's not likely, given advances in medicine and fitness. In 1900, the average person could not expect to live beyond 50. When Social Security began in 1935, the retirement age of 65 was actually older than the roughly 61 years the average male could expect to live. Today, Social Security recipients of both sexes can expect to live at least into their 70s.

That has turned the business of retirement on its head. Now, it is about managing decades of post-labor life rather than awaiting the grim reaper. That explains why so many retirees and "pre-retirees" say they expect to work well past their nominal retirement. Indeed, the trend toward early retirement in the past decade seems to be reversing slightly. After dropping for some time to about 62, the average age of retirement has leveled off at about 63. "The word retirement is going to lose its meaning over time," says Jim Thompson, director of shareholder education for AARP's investment program at Zurich Scudder Investments.

Retirement certainly isn't the word one would use to describe Sharon Dunn's lifestyle. The resident of Sun City Grand, an upscale community of people 50 and older developed by Del Webb Corp., builder of the pioneering Sun City retirement community in Phoenix 41 years ago, defies easy categorization. Dunn, 51, retired early from her job as a facilities maintenance manager at Los Alamos National Laboratory in New Mexico. She moved to Arizona, where she intended to look for another job. But, she says with a laugh, "I haven't had the time."

No wonder. As she tells it, "My calendar just fills up." There's golf two or three times a week, bicycling, and hiking nearby mountain trails. "I was terrified of retiring," she says. "My life was my job; I worked 10 to 12 hours a day. I had no idea how much I disliked it." And her new life? "It's like being a kid again. Either I'll go back to school, or I'll look for a new job."

Redefining Retirement Communities

Satisfying the multiple interests of the zoomers is a marketing challenge. The cookie-cutter prescription of the retirement communities of the 1960s doesn't hold much appeal for zoomers, who as expressive adolescents spray-painted psychedelic images on the sides of their VW buses. Nor do a golf course, swimming pool, and tennis court suffice as amenities. Today's "active adult" communities have gyms that would put most college athletic programs to shame, computer labs with high-speed Internet access, and meeting rooms where local universities often hold special courses. And even the notion of moving to some Sun Belt locale is losing its shine. It's a pretty picture except for one big cloud: Most of these aging baby boomers are blissfully unaware—or maybe just unwilling to acknowledge—what it might mean to live 30 or 40 years beyond the day they quit their day jobs. This will be a time when they may be caring for adolescent children and aging parents at the same moment because they delayed having children, and because their own parents are living longer. "There is horrendous denial about the issue of aging," says Christopher Hayes, a Long Island University professor who studies boomer retirement trends. "My feeling is the first wave is going to get hit in the breadbasket in the next five to 10 years. The reality is the BMW is going to have to be downsized to a Beetle."

Scratch the surface of the statistics, and you begin to peel at the hidden anxiety. It's not just the recent implosion of the retirement savings plans that many are counting on to finance their retirement. Even though marketers paint a glorious picture of active zoomers retiring early, the reality can be quite different. According to a paper delivered [in 2000] at a Metropolitan Life [Insurance Co.] retirement conference, the No. 1 reason cited for retiring earlier than planned was bad health or disability. "The thing I worry about is health," says Ralph Hegreness, who sold a computer-consulting company in Bellevue, Wash., and relocated to a new multigenerational community in the high desert north of Phoenix. "I feel quite vulnerable along that line. We're paying $560 a month for health insurance." He works out vigorously, hits the gym regularly, or just jogs in the neighborhood. No company illustrates this shift more than Del Webb. "We're seeing these people coming younger and wealthier and healthier than their parents," says the vice president of market research, Paul Bessler. In the early '90s, the median annual retirement income of Sun City buyers was between $35,000 and $40,000, says Bessler, and median net worth was between $400,000 and $500,000. Now, the median income is between $60,000 and $80,000, and net worth between $700,000 and $1 million.

Retiring Younger and Richer

The changing demographics have led Del Webb and other developers to build more-luxurious homes and to emphasize lifestyle over location. Prior generations "viewed retirement as an ending," Bessler says. "What I am seeing [today] is just the opposite: 'Now it's my turn. I'm just beginning life.'"

Another change: a more youthful clientele, coupled with second careers in retirement, has spawned a demand for new amenities. One of the most popular options at Del Webb's multigenerational community outside Phoenix is "La Casita"—a separate, in-law suite often used for a home office.

Entertainment rooms and wine cellars are also in demand. "They've always put an emphasis on lifestyle issues, and that will be reflected in retirement, too," says Wake Forest University Prof. Charles Longino.

An expert on retiree migration, Longino has detected changes in the pattern of retiree living. In addition to Florida, popular destinations nowadays for retirees are the mountainous areas of the West (Utah, Nevada, Colorado) and smaller states in the South (Tennessee, the Carolinas, Arkansas). Among the places where the retiree population is growing fastest: Henderson, Nev.; Park City, Utah; Prescott, Ariz.; and Georgetown, Texas. What many of these places offer, somewhat ironically for mobile boomers who have lived life on Internet time, is a sense of community and a slower pace. "Our analysis shows that the fastest-growing elderly populations tend to be in smaller and medium-sized metropolitan areas in the 'new West' and 'new South,'" says Frey. Another phenomenon, as boomers stay put and age, is the graying of once-hippie havens like Burlington, Vt.; Madison, Wis.; and Boulder, Colo.

Today's 'active adult' communities have gyms that would put most college athletic programs to shame.

Some aging boomers with adolescent or younger children still at home, or with elderly parents, are opting to stay put. In some cases, one half of a retired couple may still be working. To accommodate these folks, Del Webb built its first "four-season" retirement community not far from Chicago in Huntley, Ill. Huntley is where retired TWA flight attendant Carolyn Kleen, 58, and her husband, Jim, 61, a high school art teacher, moved to in June 1999 from nearby Elgin. "We have family here and love the change of seasons," says Carolyn, who takes line-dancing classes and belongs to the Prairie Singers chorus.

Jim's mother, 90, was "a major factor in staying nearby," says Carolyn.

Caregiving Comes Full Circle

Caring for one's parents in one's own retirement—now that may be the perfect boomer irony. A generation that has defied its age with herbal tonics and exercise comes face to face with it.

Ah, but not too soon. For now, let's do as 56-year-old Barbara Lawson does. Up at 5 a.m. for her exercise regime, the Arizona transplant (she moved to suburban Phoenix from Texas after the death of her husband and the loss of a corporate job) is, as she joyfully decrees, "on the cusp" of being a boomer. The former corporate health manager has her own company teaching seniors how to stretch and do strength-training. "I am a boomer by psychology," she says in her own age-defying way. "Now, I am ready to reinvent myself."

She—and 78 million others.

The Elderly Contribute to Society

David Gould

David Gould is editor and researcher at Parliament House, a publishing company in Canberra, Australia. He wrote this piece for the Age, *one of Australia's oldest daily newspapers.*

There is a particular fairy tale that you can tell to your children. It runs as follows. "Once upon a time, there was a rich and prosperous land. However, most of the people who lived there were becoming old. As they did so, they drained their country's treasury until there was nothing left. They spent their final years in poverty and misery, passing on to their few children an economic wasteland."

Since statisticians started drawing the obvious conclusions from our demographic profile, Australia's ageing population has been couched in terms of crisis, looming, pending or coming.

It is that terror of the age. Seniors have not saved enough to support themselves and the "pre-seniors" are saving even less. Our social security system will not survive the demands placed on it, leaving many elderly people in abject poverty. Our health care system stands at the brink of ruin, with epidemics of dementia, Alzheimer's, diabetes and other illnesses most common in old age just around the corner.

Worse still, the social security and health systems will be called on to provide decades of support, where previously only a few years on the pension in a home or hospital were required.

The only questions left, apparently, are whether the disaster can be averted and, if so, how.

But what if we have got too far ahead of ourselves? What if the question yet to be answered is this one: is there really a crisis?

An Opportunity Rather than a Crisis

There is no doubt that the population is ageing. Birth rates have been falling for the past 20 years and, with the baby boomers now closing in fast on 60, the median age—the age which exactly half the population is older and younger than—of Australians has risen by five years in the same period.

A higher percentage of our population is aged 65 or over than at any point in our history, and the figure is going to get higher. Recent research suggests that many people alive today can expect to live to 100 or beyond.

And yet while the percentage of older people in our general population has increased significantly over the past 20 years, the number of hospital beds taken up by those aged 65 or over has not increased at all. Our medical system may well be under pressure but older people are clearly not responsible.

Further, people are living longer but they are also living longer healthier. Even though people are living on average five more years, that does not equate to five more economically damaging years of hospital treatment.

As people are going to be healthier longer, they are going to be contributing to society—and the economy—for longer.

To the contrary: they have more productive years than they had previously; indeed, a greater proportion of a person's life will be spent contributing to the economy. Someone who lives until they are 75 with five years of ill health does less good for the economy than someone who lives until they are 80 with five years of ill health.

OK, so maybe the crisis facing our health system because of the ageing of the population has been a little overblown. But what about social security and superannuation? There, surely, real disaster threatens—doesn't it? Perhaps, but do not hold your breath waiting for the calamity.

Healthy people contributing to society, either by working longer or volunteering in community building activities, put more onto the economy's bottom line than they take out. As people are going to be healthier longer, they are going to be contributing to society—and to the economy—for longer.

People will work longer and thus build superannuation and savings for longer. When they do retire they will be likely to have a similar length of retirement as now, but with five or more extra years of savings. Disregarding any extra amount paid in over that period—which could be substantial, because many people are on their highest salary immediately before retirement—at a modest growth rate of 3 per cent above inflation, this provides an increase in retirement savings of close to 16 percent. Thus living longer will mean that you live better when you do retire.

Remain Skeptical of Doomsayers

So when you next read an article suggesting that aged care and health services for aged people will be costing 7 per cent of GDP [gross domestic product] by 2045 or some similar notion, ask yourself this: what is the claim based on and how does the claim compare with today? Are they taking into account the fact that older people will be healthier? Are they taking into account the fact that they will be working longer and thus less dependent on the pension?

Listen to what the doomsayers say, but do not take what they say for granted. Far from an ageing crisis, there is an ageing opportunity facing us—the opportunity for longer, healthier and wealthier lives. At the same time, the nation's economy will grow and benefits will flow to Australians of all ages.

The myth of an ageing crisis might be a bogeyman capable of frightening children. But it is no more than that.

CHAPTER 2

Does Health Care Meet the Needs of the Elderly?

Chapter Preface

When people think of long-term care for the elderly, they often think of nursing homes. Rather than live in a nursing home or other facility, however, most older adults want to "age in place," to remain in their own homes as they age. Many elderly people who would otherwise be institutionalized can remain in their homes if they receive help with such activities as bathing and dressing, using the bathroom, making meals, doing housekeeping and laundry, and going shopping. According to the National Association of Home Care, about 7.6 million people received some form of home care in 2005, and the demand for in-home services is expected to double by 2050 as the baby boom generation ages.

Not only is aging in place the preference of most elderly people, but several studies over the past three decades show that in-home care is cheaper on a per-person basis than nursing home care. The U.S. Supreme Court also favors aging in place. In a 1999 ruling known as the *Olmstead* decision, the Court ruled that elderly and disabled people should be able to live in their own community in the least restrictive setting possible. The *Olmstead* decision mandates that federal and state policies shift away from the institutionalization of the elderly toward more home-based care. One of several controversies in the elderly health care debate is whether the federal government will be able to effectively implement the *Olmstead* decision directive.

Despite the U.S. Supreme Court's ruling and the studies that support it, current public policies still favor the institutionalization of the elderly. According to the National Association of Area Agencies on Aging (N4A), the umbrella organization for the 655 area agencies on aging in the United States, "federal policy does not adequately recognize that the most cost-effective form of long-term care is provided through home and community-based services." Indeed, more than 80 percent of the money spent on long-term care in the United States each year goes to nursing homes, even though it costs significantly less to care for the elderly in their own home.

One reason for the continued reliance on institutionalization is that the government's two health care programs do not pay for in-home care. Medicare, the federal government's health insurance program for the elderly and disabled, pays for only thirty days in a nursing home and will not pay for long-term home care at all. As a result, many middle-class seniors are forced to spend down their savings until they reach the poverty level, at which time they can qualify for Medicaid, the government's health insurance program for poor people. Although Medicaid pays about 60 percent of the nation's annual nursing home costs, it does not pay for in-home assistance, with the exception of a few demonstration projects.

To address the dearth of home-care benefits, N4A contends that "a comprehensive national policy that shifts the focus *and* funding of long-term care to community-based services is essential to meet the needs and address the desires of America's aging population." However, many observers maintain that such a change is unlikely. Medicare and Medicaid both face financial problems and are under great strain to meet the needs of the growing elderly population. Experts generally agree that neither program is likely to expand its offerings to include in-home care anytime soon. In the absence of a policy shift, these experts encourage middle-class individuals to purchase long-term care (LTC) insurance so that they can pay for in-home help when the time comes. The authors in the following chapter discuss these health care options and other controversies in the elderly health care debate.

Medicare Reforms Have Improved Health Care for the Elderly

George W. Bush

George W. Bush is the forty-third president of the United States.

Editor's Note: President Bush delivered these remarks on Medicare to the U.S. Department of Health and Human Services in Washington, D.C., on June 16, 2005.

Forty years ago—think about that, 40 years ago this summer [2005], President Lyndon Baines Johnson, from the great state of Texas signed a law creating Medicare to guarantee health care for seniors and Americans with disabilities. In the decades since that historic act, Medicare has spared millions of our citizens from needless suffering and hardship. Medicare is a landmark achievement of a compassionate society; it is a basic trust that our government will always honor.

Medicare has also faced challenges. For decades, medicine advanced rapidly and grew to include innovations like prescription drugs—but Medicare didn't keep pace. As a result, Medicare recipients were left with a program based on the medicine of the 1960s. For example, Medicare would pay $28,000 for ulcer surgery—but not $500 for prescription drugs that eliminate the cause of most ulcers. Medicare would pay more than $100,000 to treat the effects of a stroke—but not $1,000 for a blood-thinning drug that could prevent strokes. That's an outdated system and it made no sense for American seniors. It made no sense for Americans with disabilities. And it made no sense for American taxpayers.

George W. Bush, "President Discusses New Medicare Prescription Drug Benefit," wwww.whitehouse.gov, June 16, 2005.

Medicare Reform Was Long in Coming

Year after year, politicians pledged to reform Medicare—but the job never got done—until 2003, when members of both political parties came together to deliver the greatest advance in health care for seniors since the founding of Medicare. This new law is bringing preventive medicine, better health care choices, and prescription drugs to every American receiving Medicare. The Medicare Modernization Act renewed the promise of Medicare for the 21st century—and I was honored and proud to sign that piece of legislation.

[In 2005], millions of Americans have started to benefit from the new Medicare program. Every senior entering Medicare is now eligible for a "Welcome to Medicare" physical. It's a fundamental improvement and it makes a lot of sense. Medicare patients and doctors are now able to work together to diagnose health care and health concerns right away. And there's a simple reason—the sooner you diagnose a problem, you can treat problems before they become worse. Medicare now covers preventive screenings that can catch illness from diabetes to heart disease. Medicare is covering innovative programs to help seniors with chronic diseases like high blood pressure. I urge every senior to take advantage of these new benefits in Medicare.

[The Medicare Modernization Act] is bringing preventive medicine, better health care choices, and prescription drugs to every American receiving Medicare.

In the 21st century, preventing and treating illness requires prescription drugs. Seniors know this—yet because Medicare did not cover prescription drugs, many seniors had to make painful sacrifices to pay for medicine. In my travels around the country, I met seniors who faced the agonizing choice between buying prescription drugs and buying groceries. I met retirees who resorted to cutting pills in half. I met Americans who were forced to spend their retirement years working just to pay for their prescriptions. These hardships undermined the basic promise of Medicare—and thanks to the Medicare Modernization Act, those days are coming to an end.

To provide immediate help with drug costs, the new Medicare law created drug discount cards. [In 2005,] millions of seniors have used these cards to save billions of dollars. In Missouri, I met a woman who used her discount card to buy $10 worth of drugs for $1.14. She was happy with the card. Another senior went to her pharmacy and spent under $30 for medicine that used to cost about four times as much. And here is what she said: "When he got out my medicine card and told me what the savings was, I about dropped my false teeth."

All Medicare Beneficiaries Will Receive Drug Benefits

The Medicare Modernization Act created a prescription drug benefit to replace drug discount cards and bring savings and peace of mind to all 42 million Medicare beneficiaries. The new benefit will help every senior, as well as Americans with developmental and physical disabilities and mental illness and HIV/AIDS. Congress scheduled the prescription drug benefit to start in January of 2006. Thanks to the leadership of Secretary [Mike] Leavitt and Mark McClellan, we are on track to deliver prescription drug coverage on time to every American senior.

As Medicare's professional staff prepares to implement the prescription drug benefit, we also must ensure that seniors are ready to take full advantage of their new opportunities. And that's why I've come here today. It's important for everyone to understand that Medicare prescription drug coverage is voluntary. Seniors can choose to take advantage of the benefit, or they can choose not to. It's up to them.

And there's plenty of time to make the decision. Starting on October [1, 2005], Medicare beneficiaries will begin getting information about the new prescription drug plans available. They will receive a handbook called, "Medicare and You," that includes detailed information about their options. If they like what they see and choose to get prescription drug coverage, they can enroll anytime between November 15th [of 2005] and May 15th of [2006]. Beneficiaries should make their decisions as soon as they are ready, because enrolling before May will ensure that they pay the lowest possible premiums.

The federal government will work hard to ensure that Medicare beneficiaries understand their options. I've asked every agency that touches the lives of seniors or disabled Americans to devote resources to explaining the prescription drug benefit. And we need the help of people in the private sector, as well. The only way to reach everyone on Medicare is to mobilize compassionate citizens in communities all over the country. . . . We will unite a wide range of Americans—from doctors, to nurses, to pharmacists, to state and local leaders, to seniors groups, to disability advocates, to faith-based organizations. Together, we will work to ensure that every American on Medicare is ready to make a confident choice about prescription drug coverage, so they can finally receive the modern health care they deserve.

As we spread the word about the new opportunities in Medicare, we will make it clear that prescription drug coverage will provide greater peace of mind for beneficiaries in three key ways.

Seniors with the Highest Costs Will Get the Most Help

First, the new Medicare coverage will provide greater peace of mind by helping all seniors and Americans with disabilities pay for prescription drugs—no matter how they pay for medicine now. On average, Medicare beneficiaries will receive more than $1,300 in federal assistance to pay for prescription drugs. Seniors with no drug coverage and average prescription expenses will see their drug bills reduced by half or more. The new Medicare benefits will also provide special help for seniors with the highest drug costs. Starting in January [2006], Medicare will cover 95 percent of all prescription costs after a senior has spent $3,600 in a year. Seniors will never be able to predict what challenges life will bring—but thanks to Medicare, they can be certain they will never have their entire savings wiped out to pay for prescription drugs.

Second, the new Medicare coverage will provide greater peace of mind by offering beneficiaries better health care choices than they have ever had. Seniors will be able to choose any Medicare prescription drug plan that fits their needs and their medical history. Seniors who want to keep their Medicare the way it is will be able to do so. Seniors using Medicare Advantage to save money will be able to keep their plans and get better drug benefits. Seniors who receive drug coverage from a former employer or union can count on new support from Medicare to help them keep their good benefits. Every prescription drug plan will offer a broad choice of brand name drugs and generic drugs. Seniors will also have the choice to pick up their prescriptions at local pharmacies or to have the medicine delivered to their home. . . .

Medicare is now modern, reformed and compassionate.

Third, the new Medicare coverage will provide greater peace of mind by extending extra help to low-income seniors and beneficiaries with disabilities. For years, beneficiaries on the tightest budgets received no help from Medicare to pay for prescription drugs. Because we acted, about a third of American seniors will be eligible for a Medicare drug benefit that includes little or no premiums, low deductibles, and no gaps in coverage. On average, Medicare will pick up the tab for more than 95 percent of prescription drug costs for low-income seniors. To receive this important assistance, low-income seniors have to fill out a straightforward, four-page application form with, at most, 16 questions. No financial documents or complicated records are required, and the forms are easy to obtain. In fact, millions of applications have already been mailed to low-income seniors. If you or a family member receives one of these, I urge you to fill it out and send it in. . . .

An Outreach Effort Is Essential

With all of these essential reforms, the Medicare Modernization Act created a new commitment to seniors and Americans with disabilities—and all of you are helping to make good on that commitment. By lending a hand to neighbors in need, you are strengthening your communities and showing the great compassion of our country. Many organizations have already launched innovative efforts to reach seniors. And I'll continue to call on people to put forth innovative strategies to reach our seniors.

For example, in Wisconsin and Indiana, more than 270 community leaders are coming together to find ways to get information to rural seniors. In Chicago, a food pantry, the Catholic Archdiocese, and a news publication are all working to get the word out about the new Medicare benefits. The federal Department of Transportation, under the leadership of Norm Mineta, is working with local agencies to post Medicare information in buses and in highway rest stops. Thousands of pharmacies are working with Medicare to provide information for seniors. Countless other organizations are holding community events and connecting with seniors face-to-face, so Medicare recipients can get their questions answered and make informed choices about prescription drug coverage. In other words, we're on a massive education effort, starting today. And I'm asking for America's help.

You can help by making a call to your mother or father and tell them what's available. You can help by showing an older neighbor how to fill out a form. You can help by spending an afternoon at the local retirement home. And by the way, when you help somebody, you're really helping yourself. You can get information 24 hours a day calling 1-800-MEDICARE. It's pretty easy to remember, 1-800-MEDICARE. Or you can use the Internet to visit the official Medicare website at medicare.gov. All you've got to do is type in "medicare.gov" and you're going to find out what I'm talking about. . . .

I think the passage of the Medicare Modernization Act is a good lesson for all of us who work in [Washington, D.C.] You know, it wasn't all that long ago the leaders who talked about Medicare reform faced a lot of name-calling—to say the least. When Congress finally rose above politics and fulfilled its duty to America's seniors, it showed what's possible in Washington, D.C. We need that same spirit—I mean, this bill is proof that Americans really aren't interested in seeing one party win and another party lose. What Americans want to see is people coming together to solve problems, that's what they want to see. We had a problem in Medicare—it wasn't working the way it should; it wasn't modern, it wasn't answering the needs of our seniors. And by coming together, we have done our job here in Washington. And as a result of working together, we have changed Medicare for the better. Medicare is now modern, reformed and compassionate. And I urge all seniors—all seniors and those folks here in America who want to help seniors, look into this new prescription drug benefit; it will make your life better.

Medicaid Eligibility Requirements Protect the Elderly Poor

Ellen O'Brien

Ellen O'Brien is a research associate professor at the Georgetown University Health Policy Institute.

One of the most persistent questions in U.S. social policy concerns the mix of personal and public responsibility for long-term care. Although most long-term care is provided by family members on an unpaid basis, most of the nation's long-term care spending (three-fourths) is concentrated on nursing home care, and Medicaid, the nation's health care program for poor and low-income Americans, is the largest source of payment for that care. Nearly half of the nation's nursing home bill was paid by Medicaid in 2003, while just over a quarter was paid out-of-pocket, and less than 10 percent was covered by private insurance. For some, this distribution of financial responsibility raises concerns about who is, and who should be, paying for long-term care. Most especially, critics contend that Medicaid has been stretched beyond its original purpose of providing a safety net for the poor, and has evolved into a middle class entitlement and an asset shelter for the rich.

The Nation's Safety Net

As the nation's safety net for long-term care, Medicaid provides assistance to the poor, and to those who are impoverished by high medical and long-term care spending. To be eligible for Medicaid assistance with the costs of nursing home care, individuals must have limited assets, and must contribute all of their available income toward the cost of that care. The widows who make up the bulk of the nation's nursing home population must reduce their "countable" assets to $2,000 or below, and contribute all of their monthly income (with the exception of a $30 to $90 "personal needs allowance") toward the cost of their care. Special rules allow married couples to set aside income and assets for a community spouse (within federal guidelines), but many states allow community spouses to keep only the federal minimum levels of income ($1,561 per month) and assets ($19,020)—hardly enough assets to assure financial security in retirement.

Medicaid, the nation's health care program for poor and low-income Americans, is the largest source of payment for [nursing home care].

Although the law requires Medicaid beneficiaries to contribute or spend down their income and assets, critics [such as Stephen A. Moses] contend that "impoverishment is a fallacy" and that Medicaid pays for the care of most nursing home residents because people with the resources to afford their own care—middle-income and wealthier people, even "millionaires"—transfer their assets to qualify for public subsidies intended for the poor. Critics argue that a veritable cottage industry of elder-law attorneys has sprung up whose mission is to advise clients with sizable assets about how they can preserve those assets and get Medicaid to pay for nursing home care when they need it. They claim that, rather than spending down (actually impoverishing themselves), the elderly hire estate-planning lawyers and artificially impoverish themselves by establishing trusts, giving cash gifts to children and grandchildren, or otherwise concealing their ability to pay for their own care by converting countable assets to exempt forms (by spending assets on a car or on a home or home renovation, since those assets are not counted in making a Medicaid eligibility determination). Federal law imposes a penalty period (denying Medicaid eligibility for a period of time) for those who shelter or divest assets for the purpose of qualifying for Medicaid, but critics say those penalties are avoided—in whole or in part—by those who get good legal advice.

As the nation's safety net for long-term care, Medicaid provides assistance to ... those ... impoverished by high medical and long-term care spending.

This reliance on Medicaid, the critics suggest, creates a number of short-term and long-term problems. In the near term, they claim that the middle- and upper-income elderly who seek Medicaid subsidies for nursing home care are drawing finite resources away from other Medicaid beneficiaries (needy children and families) by passing resources to their heirs that could have been used to pay for nursing home care. In the longer term, they argue, a middle class "sense of entitlement" to Medicaid's nursing home benefits creates a significant barrier to the expansion of private long-term care insurance and a more rational financing system for long-term care. To correct this imbalance, they advocate that Medicaid eligibility be restricted—by, for example, stiffening penalties for those who transfer assets.

Little Evidence of Abuse

Most of these claims about Medicaid's incentive effects are supported only by anecdotal accounts of abuses by the rich. Empirical research paints a very different picture. Research demonstrates that a large proportion of the disabled elderly in the community (who are at risk of nursing home placement) have limited assets. Many qualify for Medicaid in the community, and most would qualify for Medicaid at admission to a nursing home. Most of the elderly with disabilities in the community have too little wealth to warrant hiring an attorney to arrange an asset transfer. Moreover, studies that look at who pays for nursing home care find that, even though they have limited resources, a large proportion of the elderly pay their own way throughout their nursing home stays, and that the elderly are less likely to rely on Medicaid than would be predicted given their resources.

There is little evidence that large numbers of the elderly are planning their estates for the purpose of gaining easy access to Medicaid in the event they need nursing home care. There is no evidence that they use transfers or trusts to significantly shift cost burdens to Medicaid, and little evidence that those who do transfer sizable assets gain eligibility for Medicaid. Furthermore, there is little evidence that Medicaid interferes with saving for future needs, or that it prevents people from purchasing private long-term care insurance. The elderly who expect to need nursing home care—and especially those of modest financial means who are likely to qualify for Medicaid—save more not less than those who do not expect to use nursing home care. Finally, generous Medicaid eligibility explains very little of the very low demand for private long-term care insurance.

This paper reviews the empirical evidence on the prevalence and magnitude of asset transfers to achieve Medicaid eligibility, and the evidence on whether Medicaid's means-testing creates a disincentive to save or purchase private long-term care insurance.

Do the Elderly Transfer Assets to Qualify for Medicaid?

In theory, Medicaid's means-testing creates financial incentives for the elderly to hide or transfer their assets to obtain Medicaid eligibility. In reality, most of the elderly at risk of nursing home placement have limited resources and little reason to pursue legal advice to divest their assets.

Most of the elderly lack the financial resources to pay for extended nursing home stays. Much of this debate is fueled by the perception that the elderly are more affluent than younger households and thus less deserving of Medicaid subsidy. Most elderly households, however, are far from affluent. Although it is true that elderly households are less likely than younger households to live in poverty, the median household income of elderly Medicare beneficiaries is only about $25,000. Among elderly women living alone (those who are most likely to become nursing home residents), median household income is less than $12,000.

Few of the elderly have the ability to finance their own long-term care needs when those needs extend over many years.

The conventional wisdom also suggests that elderly households are better off financially—despite having lower incomes—because they have substantially greater wealth than younger households. In fact, although the elderly as a group have higher net worth than the nonelderly, most of the elderly are not wealthy. For many, their primary asset is their home, but their housing equity is modest. In 2000, for example, the median total wealth (financial wealth including home equity of elderly households) was just $108,885 for the elderly age 65 and older. Excluding home equity, the median net worth of elderly households was just $23,885. The elderly as a group have substantial resources, but that financial wealth is highly unevenly distributed: assets are almost nonexistent for the elderly in the bottom 30 percent of the wealth distribution, while the top 5 percent have financial wealth (excluding home equity) in excess of $300,000.

The elderly in poor health, and those with functional impairments (who need or may soon need long-term care), have even more limited financial resources than the non-disabled elderly and those in good health. The elderly in self-reported excellent health have more than three times the wealth of those in poor health; and when households in which two spouses are both in excellent health are compared to households in which both spouses are in poor health, the wealth disparity is ten to one. Studies of the disabled elderly living in the community also show that most have few assets beyond a home, and, consequently, most are financially eligible for Medicaid at admission to the nursing home, or within six months of admission. Few of the elderly have the ability to finance their own long-term care needs when those needs extend over many years.

Paying for Nursing Home Stays

Of the elderly with any nursing home use, a substantial share pay their own way. Despite limited financial resources, most elderly nursing home residents rely on private resources in part or in full to pay the costs of nursing home care. A study of the lifetime nursing home use of the elderly by Brenda Spillman and Peter Kemper reveals that 44 percent of the elderly nursing home users paid for their care using only private funds, 16 percent began as private payers, exhausted their own resources, and converted to Medicaid, and 27 percent were covered by Medicaid upon admission to the nursing home and throughout their use. (The remaining 13 percent of elderly nursing home users were covered by Medicare only or other sources.) Contrary to the critics' portrayal, a substantial share of the elderly pays their own way in full because they (or their families) have sufficient income and resources to do so. Moreover, even if they are receiving financial assistance from Medicaid, elderly nursing home residents do pay their own way to the extent that they can. Those who are covered by Medicaid are contributing all of their available income to cover the cost of their own care. The proportion of the elderly who qualify for Medicaid at admission to the nursing home is as high as it is (27 percent) because a large proportion of the disabled elderly in the community have few assets and exhaust what they do have in the community, not because they have transferred their assets.

There is little evidence that nursing home residents transfer assets to gain eligibility for Medicaid. Other research studies confirm that Medicaid-induced transfers are not widespread among current or likely nursing home residents. [Researchers] Frank Sloan and Mae Shayne find that people who have a relatively high risk of entering nursing homes (the disabled elderly) have too little wealth to warrant hiring an attorney to arrange an asset transfer. Using data from the 1989 National Long Term Care Survey, Sloan and Shayne find that the majority of the disabled elderly in the community are either already financially eligible or would become eligible for Medicaid immediately upon entering a nursing home. They found that an estimated 19 percent of the disabled elderly in the community were qualified for Medicaid in the community, and an additional 59 percent would have qualified financially for Medicaid at admission to a nursing home. The authors conclude that it is a lack of any significant wealth accumulation beyond a home that accounts for the high likelihood of qualifying for Medicaid, not asset transfers.

Further, in an analysis of the 1985 National Nursing Home Survey, Edward Norton found that nursing home residents spend down to Medicaid at a much lower rate than would be expected given their income and assets. Rather than transferring assets to become Medicaid eligible, some of the elderly may be receiving transfers from children or others, or voluntarily converting housing equity into liquid assets, to extend the period before they become Medicaid eligible. Norton concludes that there is a "strong aversion to welfare," contradicting the conventional wisdom that Medicaid's nursing home subsidy creates a strong financial incentive to divest assets.

Examining the Evidence

There is little evidence that the elderly in general transfer assets to gain Medicaid eligibility. Critics contend that the middle-class elderly may give large gifts or establish trusts to preserve their assets for heirs. Assets placed in certain kinds of trusts are not treated as financial resources available to pay for care, provided they meet certain criteria. The trust must be irrevocable (meaning the terms of the trust cannot be changed at any time), it must be established well in advance of the application for Medicaid (federal law imposes a 60-month look-back period for assets placed in trust), and the trustor may not have access to the principal, though she may receive income from the trust. However, recent analysis of empirical data reveals that trusts are established by a relatively small proportion of the elderly, and mostly for purposes other than establishing eligibility for Medicaid. . . .

Few Medicaid Applicants Have Transferred Assets

Audits of Medicaid applications also reveal that only a small fraction of individuals who applied for Medicaid, and an even smaller share of those found eligible for Medicaid, transfer assets for the purpose of qualifying for free care under Medicaid. In 1993, the U.S. General Accounting Office (GAO) reviewed more than 400 applications for Medicaid nursing home assistance in Massachusetts (a state thought to have a high level of estate planning). The GAO found that only a small fraction of applicants (1 in 8) had transferred assets (the average amount transferred was $46,000). Further, about half of the applicants who had transferred assets were subsequently denied eligibility for Medicaid. A significantly larger share of

Medicaid applicants, 50 percent, had *converted* countable assets to exempt forms. Typically, they used "excess" assets to prepay funeral expenses. The amount of assets protected in this way, however, was very small ($4,700 on average).

Stricter Rules Would Save Little

Reforms designed to curb asset transfers would produce only small Medicaid savings. Estimates of the likely impact of policy proposals to further restrict asset transfers also suggest that there is not a significant asset transfer problem. . . .

States have also estimated the cost saving potential of restricting asset transfers. Three states have submitted waiver proposals to the Centers for Medicare and Medicaid Services proposing to substantially increase the penalties for asset transfers. By their own estimates, however, the impact on Medicaid expenditures would be small, with estimated savings (over a five-year demonstration period) of 0.6 percent of Medicaid nursing home expenditures in Massachusetts and 1.4 percent in Connecticut.

Medicaid is what it was intended to be, a safety net for those who cannot afford to pay for long-term care.

A proposal in the President's 2006 budget to tighten rules concerning asset transfers has also been estimated to produce only modest Medicaid savings over 10 years. The Office of Management and Budget estimates that federal Medicaid outlays would be reduced by $4.5 billion between 2006 and 2015—a reduction of less than two-tenths of one percent in projected federal Medicaid expenditures. State expenditures would also be reduced by an estimated $3.4 billion. . . .

Medicaid Remains a Safety Net

The argument that something needs to be done about abuses of the Medicaid eligibility rules is not supported by the facts.

The studies reviewed in this paper do not support the claim that asset transfers are widespread or costly to Medicaid, or that restricting Medicaid eligibility would substantially increase savings or purchases of private long-term care insurance. Certainly, some Medicaid planning for nursing home care occurs. Some families try to protect modest assets (and, very infrequently, substantial assets) for future needs or for inheritances. But policy reforms designed to close down remaining loopholes are not going to make much of a dent in Medicaid's nursing home spending because most people who end up on Medicaid are already paying what they can. The fact is that Medicaid is what it was intended to be, a safety net for those who cannot afford to pay for long-term care.

Long-Term Care Insurance Meets the Needs of the Elderly

Richard W. Johnson and Cori E. Uccello

Richard W. Johnson and Cori E. Uccello are research associates at the Center for Retirement Research at Boston College. Johnson is also a principal research associate, and Uccello is a consultant at the Urban Institute, a nonpartisan economic and social policy research organization.

As the population ages, more Americans than ever before will need long-term care [LTC]. The cost of providing services is already straining government and family budgets, and costs are expected to soar in a few decades when the Baby Boomers begin to reach their 80s. One option often touted as a possible solution to the looming crisis is to promote private insurance coverage of long-term care needs. . . .

Long-term care encompasses a wide range of services for people who need assistance on a regular basis because of chronic illness or physical or mental disabilities. Unlike most health services, long-term care is not generally designed to treat an illness or condition. Although it can include skilled nursing care, it consists primarily of help with basic activities of daily living (such as bathing, eating, dressing, and using the toilet) and with tasks necessary for independent living (such as shopping, cooking, and housework). Although two-fifths of long-term care recipients are under the age of 65, this brief focuses on services provided to older Americans.

Older people with the most serious disabilities generally receive round-the-clock care in nursing homes. Only about 5 percent of Medicare enrollees age 65 and older, or about 1.6 million seniors, resided in nursing homes in 2002. However,

44 percent of 65-year-olds can expect to live in a nursing home now or at some point in the future.

Most long-term care recipients live in their own homes or with their families. About 1.3 million seniors in the community receive care from paid helpers, who provide skilled home care or unskilled care with basic personal activities. Another 5.5 million older Americans in the community receive unpaid help from family members. The burden on family caregivers of juggling work and other responsibilities is likely to grow in the future as women—who provide most family care—continue to spend more time in the labor force.

Who Pays for Long-Term Care?

The cost of long-term care services, especially nursing home care, can be staggering. In 2004, the average daily private pay rate for a private room in a nursing home was $192, or about $78,100 annually. A semi-private room was nearly as expensive, at $169 per day, or $61,700 for the year. Home health aides who provide assistance with personal care activities charged $18 per hour on average in 2004. At three hours per day, five days per week, annual home care costs would total more than $14,000.

The nation spent an estimated $135 billion on long-term care for the aged in 2004, devoting 68 percent to care in nursing homes and 32 percent to home-based care. Medicaid paid for 35 percent of all long-term care spending on older Americans, Medicare covered 25 percent of costs, private health insurance paid another 4 percent, and care recipients and their families paid out of pocket for 33 percent of costs (see Figure 1).

For those who qualify, Medicaid covers nursing home care, home health services, and non-medical home- and community-based care designed to enable persons with disabilities to remain in the community. The program pays for about 39 percent of all care received in nursing homes by the aged and 25 percent of care received at home. However, individuals must meet strict income and asset tests to qualify. Eligibility rules are complex and vary by state. Some states use the federal thresholds for receipt of Supplemental Security Income (SSI) to determine Medicaid eligibility, which in 2005 are $579 per month in countable income and $2,000 in countable assets for unmarried people. In other states, Medicaid pays for long-term care services for individuals with incomes up to 300 percent of the federal SSI threshold.

As the population ages, more Americans than ever before will need long-term care.

People with too much wealth or income to qualify initially for Medicaid can receive benefits once they have spent nearly all of their resources on long-term care services. According to one estimate, about one-third of nursing home residents ineligible for Medicaid when they are admitted deplete enough of their assets to qualify for coverage before they are discharged. Most states allow Medicaid applicants to subtract medical and long-term care expenses from income before determining eligibility, enabling people with high long-term care bills to get on Medicaid even if their Social Security and pension incomes exceed eligibility thresholds.

Medicare is the principal payer of skilled home health services for older Americans, but coverage of other long-term care services is limited. It does not pay for any non-medical home care, and covers only temporary stays in skilled nursing facilities that follow hospitalizations. Overall, Medicare funded 42 percent of the paid care older Americans received at home in 2004 and 17 percent of the care they received in nursing homes.

Much of the financial burden of long-term care falls on care recipients and their families. Individuals without private supplemental insurance who do not qualify for Medicaid must

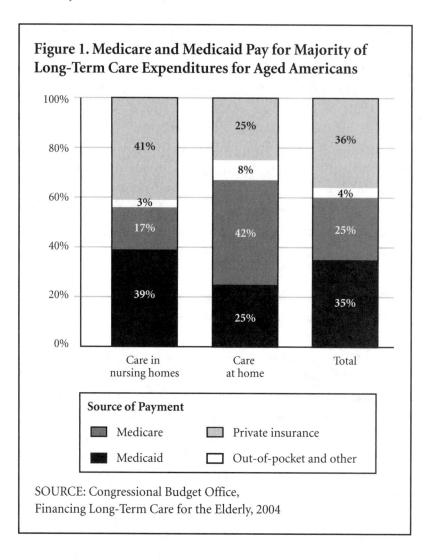

Figure 1. Medicare and Medicaid Pay for Majority of Long-Term Care Expenditures for Aged Americans

SOURCE: Congressional Budget Office, Financing Long-Term Care for the Elderly, 2004

bear the cost of Medicare deductibles and co-payments, and the entire cost of services that Medicare does not cover. Private long-term care insurance, a relatively recent insurance product, funds only 3 percent of nursing home costs for older adults and 8 percent of home health costs. Increasing private insurance coverage may reduce financial pressures on public programs and protect families from the catastrophic financial consequences of long-term care.

How Does Private Long-Term Care Insurance Work?

Like traditional medical insurance, private long-term care insurance is a financial contract whereby the insurer agrees to provide covered benefits in exchange for regular premium payments by the policyholder. The long-term care insurance market has grown steadily over the past 20 years. First sold as nursing home insurance in the 1970s, it now covers a wide range of services, including home care, adult day care, and assisted living, in addition to nursing home care. The cumulative number of long-term care insurance policies purchased has increased from fewer than 1 million in 1987 to over 9 million by the end of 2002, but still covers only a small share of the population.

Long-term care insurance can be purchased through either the individual or group market. Group plans are typically sponsored, but not subsidized, by employers. Individual policies continue to dominate the market, but employer-sponsored plans are growing rapidly, fueled in part by the creation of the Federal Long-Term Care Insurance Program in 2002, which allows federal employees, retirees, and some of their family members to purchase coverage through the federal government. About one-third of new policies sold in 2002 were sponsored by employers. By contrast, only 18 percent of policies ever sold by 2002 were employer-sponsored plans.

The cost and adequacy of policies vary by the types of services they cover, when they start paying benefits, how much they pay, and for how long. About three-quarters of individual policies purchased today cover both nursing homes and home care. In 1990, by contrast, nearly two-thirds of policies sold covered only nursing home care.

Policyholders cannot collect benefits until their disabilities reach the levels specified in their contracts. Nearly all plans now sold use the triggers specified in the Health Insurance Portability and Accountability Act of 1996 (HIPAA) to qualify for tax breaks. These plans require that beneficiaries need substantial assistance with at least two out of six activities of daily living and that their disabilities are expected to last 90 or more days, or that they need regular supervision because of severe cognitive impairment.

About three quarters of all individual plans purchased in 2000 also delay benefits for a period of time after the onset of a qualified disability. More than two-thirds of plans that delayed benefits required policyholders to wait between 90 and 100 days. Only 4 percent stipulated waiting periods longer than 100 days.

Increasing private [long-term care] insurance coverage may reduce financial pressures on public programs and protect families from the catastrophic financial consequences of long-term care.

Policies limit how much they pay for each day of care and for how long. The average daily benefit for both nursing home and community-based care was about $100 for individual policies purchased in 2000. Since policyholders often purchase coverage decades before they receive benefits, the growth in nominal long-term care costs can erode the value of the policy over time. Only about 4 in 10 new policyholders in 2000 purchased inflation protection, although the rate was higher at relatively young ages. Inflation protection generally takes the form of a fixed percentage increase per year, typically 3 or 5 percent, so some policyholders may end up with less coverage than they expected if prices of long-term care services rise especially rapidly. In addition, rather than providing lifetime benefits, about two-thirds of individual policies pay benefits for only a limited number of years, generally between two and five years.

In addition to charging higher premiums for more comprehensive plans, insurance companies generally price policies based on the age and health of the policyholder at the time of issue. Premiums do not generally differ by gender, even though women tend to use more long-term-care services than men. Some plans offer discounts to married policyholders, especially when their spouses are also covered.

Most insurers classify applicants into three broad health categories: preferred, standard, and substandard. Policies are guaranteed renewable, and rates cannot rise in response to declining health. Instead, premiums remain fixed in nominal terms over the life of the contract. However, premiums can rise for an entire class of policyholders if insurers can demonstrate that their costs exceed premium revenue, and rate increases have been common in recent years.

Premiums increase rapidly with age at issue. The average annual premium in 2002 for a policy providing up to four years of benefits, with a $150 daily benefit and a 90-day waiting period but no inflation protection, was $422 among 40-year-old purchasers. The average annual premium for the same policy was $564 at age 50, $1,337 at age 65, and $5,330 at age 79. For policies purchased at ages 40 and 50, inflation protection that increases benefits by 5 percent per year, compounded annually, more than doubles the annual premium. For coverage purchased at age 79, inflation protection increases premiums by less than half.

About 9 percent of adults ages 55 and older (or 5.3 million people) had private long-term care insurance coverage in 2002. Only 7 percent of those ages 55 to 64 had coverage, but coverage rates among the working-age population are likely to increase as more employers offer long-term care insurance. Men are just as likely to report coverage as women, even though they are less likely to use long-term care services.

The likelihood of private long-term care coverage increases with income and wealth, because affluent adults can better afford insurance premiums and they would have to deplete their assets to qualify for Medicaid. Only 3 percent of older adults with incomes below $20,000 and 4 percent with financial assets below $20,000 had coverage in 2002, compared with 14 percent of older adults with incomes above $50,000 and 18 percent of those with financial assets above $100,000. More than half of policyholders had incomes exceeding $50,000 or financial assets exceeding $100,000.

What Are the Advantages of Private Insurance?

Raising private long-term care coverage rates and reducing the current reliance on Medicaid could improve the efficiency and fairness of long-term care financing. Medicaid imposes a 100 percent tax on most assets for those who receive long-term care through the program, penalizing those who save for their old age. The savings rate in the United States is notoriously low, and most Americans do not accumulate much non-housing wealth outside of Social Security and employer-sponsored pension plans. By requiring policyholders to set aside funds in the form of premium payments each year, private insurance can raise national savings and thus promote economic growth.

Unlike private long-term care insurance, Medicaid is not designed to protect the assets of those receiving long-term care services. It leaves them with nothing to pass on to their heirs and impoverishes those who return to the community after temporary nursing home stays. Recent Medicaid reforms have increased the level of income and assets that are reserved for spouses, in an effort to provide better financial security for the community-dwelling husbands and wives of nursing home residents. However, these reforms do not appear to have substantially improved the economic security of spouses remaining in the community.

Another disadvantage of the current system is that Medicaid tends to distort the choice between home- and institutional-based care. Most older adults prefer to remain in their own homes, instead of moving to nursing homes. But despite recent improvements, Medicaid rules still make it difficult for frail older adults to receive subsidized care at home. Federal law stipulates that special Medicaid initiatives to provide home- and community-based services to people with disabilities must not increase Medicaid spending, forcing states to limit eligibility for these services and impose other requirements to keep costs down. As a result, some Medicaid enrollees cannot afford to remain in the community because the monthly stipend that the program allows is too small to cover their living expenses.

The current system also imposes substantial burdens on state governments. Medicaid is a joint federal-state program, with the federal government paying a majority of the costs. Nonetheless, states end up financing a sizable portion of Medicaid expenses. Medicaid now consumes more resources than any other single item in overall state budgets, including elementary and secondary education. Long-term care services for the aged accounted for 19 percent of all Medicaid spending in 2002, a share that is likely to rise in the future as the population ages. Increases in private long-term care insurance coverage could reduce the strain on state Medicaid programs.

Medicare Should Be Reformed

Jessica Mittler

Jessica Mittler is a senior health research analyst at Mathematica Policy Research, a nonpartisan organization that conducts policy research and surveys in health care, education, and welfare.

Health care costs have been rising rapidly for Medicare just as they have for the rest of the population. From 2000 to 2004, total Medicare benefit payments per enrollee grew at average rate of 7 percent per year. Evidence on variation in Medicare spending, service use, and quality of care across geographic regions and among various types of beneficiaries point to opportunities to improve care efficiency and quality. Because Medicare is such a large share of health care spending, initiatives to improve its efficiency and the quality of care it funds will potentially influence the health care system as a whole.

How Medical Spending Is Set

Geographic. Spending per beneficiary in fee-for-service Medicare varies widely by location, suggesting inefficiency. Among urban areas, spending in 2000 ranged from $3,500 in Santa Fe, New Mexico, to about $9,200 in Miami, Florida. After adjusting for differences in the health of beneficiaries and the amount providers pay for wages, rent, and the like, researchers still find substantial spending differences resulting from variation in the use of services. Even within geographic areas, there is evidence of both overuse and underuse of services.

- Beneficiaries in high-spending geographic areas use more of some types of services, such as intensive hos-

Jessica Mittler, "Medicare: Making It a Force for Innovation and Efficiency," *Issue Brief*, July 2005. Copyright © 2005 by The Commonwealth Fund. Reproduced by permission.

pital care or specialty visits, but do not experience bet- quality of care, better outcomes, or more satisfaction than their counterparts in low-spending areas. For these kinds of services, use increases as the supply of services grows, expanding to include cases for which there is weaker evidence of the effectiveness of these services.

- Recent studies show nationwide underuse of some effective services. In one study, for example, Medicare beneficiaries were found to receive certain known, effective services less than two-thirds of the time than warranted for common conditions such as heart disease, breast cancer, diabetes, and stroke.

Medicare's challenge is to reduce the use of ineffective or inappropriate services and increase the use of appropriate and effective underutilized services. Achieving this will be complicated because consensus on the amount of care that is appropriate and the impact of the price Medicare pays for that care does not always exist.

Variations Among Beneficiaries

In any given year Medicare spending is highly concentrated among a small portion of beneficiaries. For example, in 2002 the top 5 percent of fee-for-service beneficiaries accounted for almost half of all dollars spent in fee-for-service Medicare, and the top quarter represented nearly 90 percent of all fee-for-service expenditures.

Many of the high-spenders are the chronically ill. Almost 80 percent of all beneficiaries have at least one chronic condition, but the 20 percent of beneficiaries with five or more chronic conditions account for two-thirds of Medicare spending. About one-quarter of beneficiaries with at least one of three conditions—congestive heart failure [CHF], chronic obstructive pulmonary disease, and diabetes—account for about 60 percent of Medicare's fee-for-service spending.

Not surprisingly, the chronically ill see more doctors, have more visits, have more hospital stays, and use more prescription drugs than the average beneficiary. Beneficiaries with five or more chronic conditions have more than twice as many total office visits and physicians caring for them in a year than the average beneficiary, and they have five times as many prescriptions filled than those with no chronic conditions.

Initiatives to improve [Medicare's] efficiency and the quality of care it funds will potentially influence the health care system as a whole.

Many hospitalizations among the chronically ill are preventable. The Agency for Health Care Research and Quality estimates that about 800,000 hospital admissions for beneficiaries with CHF in 1999 could have been avoided with better outpatient management of their conditions. The costs associated with these admissions totaled $4.6 billion, which was 2.3 percent of total Medicare spending ($209 billion) in 1999.

It is widely believed that the health care system and Medicare often fail to meet the complex needs of the chronically ill. The fragmented care system, and the fact that high spending beneficiaries who survive tend to remain high spenders over long periods of time, suggest that targeting care coordination interventions to this group of beneficiaries could be effective in improving the quality of their care and decreasing costs.

Strategies for Strengthening Efficiency and Quality

Many factors affect care efficiency and quality:

- the supply of services
- provider training and preferences

- local standards of care

- financial incentives for providers and beneficiaries

- patient demands for care

The precise role of each factor and how they interact is not well established. In addition, the medical system and Medicare were not designed to support care coordination or to reward quality and efficiency:

- Beneficiaries see an average of six physicians, and the mean total of prescription medications per enrollee is 4.7. These averages are heavily influenced by the chronically ill, who see many more physicians and fill more prescriptions than their healthier counterparts.

- Information sharing across providers is frequently poor, and evidence-based practices do not exist for many conditions, especially for treatment of multiple chronic conditions.

- Medicare's benefit package lacks coverage for many services needed to maintain or stabilize conditions and Medicare does not reimburse providers for care coordination activities. (An important coverage gap was filled with the addition of prescription drug coverage in 2006.)

- Multiple sources of coverage can create administrative inefficiencies for Medicare, providers and beneficiaries. Ninety percent of beneficiaries have more than one source of coverage.

Current strategies to improve the quality of care and efficiency of the program focus on getting beneficiaries to migrate to better-performing providers, or intervening more directly to encourage the system to provide higher quality, more efficient care. Some strategies try to increase information sharing overall, whereas others focus primarily on providers or beneficiaries. Some target specific diseases.

Improving Management

Disease Management. Disease management targets individuals with a specific chronic condition that is their main health problem. The aim is to prevent a decline in health and increased expensive care through prevention and early identification of problems. The targeted conditions—such as asthma, diabetes, and congestive heart failure—typically have well-established, evidence-based treatment guidelines, and patient self-care and compliance are important factors in managing the condition. Members of a targeted population tend to have a standard set of care needs.

Disease management activities are single-disease focused and commonly involve patient education, monitoring beneficiaries' conditions against standards, and coordinating care across providers. Many different entities may provide disease management services, including health plans, hospitals, provider offices, and firms specializing in disease management programs.

Medicare's challenge is to reduce the use of ineffective or inappropriate services and increase the use of appropriate and effective underutilized services.

Three-quarters of large employers reported in 2002 that they offered some form of disease management in their benefit plan for their active employees. Nearly half of all states have implemented or are implementing disease management programs for Medicaid.

Case Management. Case management programs target individuals with complex and intens[ive] care needs that put them at risk for bad outcomes and costly hospitalizations. Targeted individuals usually have complex and diverse medical and social vulnerabilities that are not addressed by existing standardized care guidelines. These programs' interventions are highly individualized and provide more intens[ive], ongoing assistance managing care. Case managers cannot rely on standard care guidelines, since these guidelines do not address multiple conditions or social needs.

Case management programs are commonplace in health plans. In the fee-for-service program, hospitals typically help patients plan for their care after discharge from the hospital (discharge planning).

Pay-for-performance. Pay-for-performance programs target providers, giving them financial rewards for providing care that improves health. Studies show that current provider payment systems often discourage quality improvement. Pay-for-performance programs vary. Some programs reward providers for meeting performance targets for preventative services (e.g., eye exams for diabetics), health outcomes (e.g., controlled blood sugar for diabetics), or consumer satisfaction. Others reward structural improvements, such as the use of electronic medical record systems or computer physician order entry systems. Some pay for services that previously were not covered, such as care coordination activities.

Two leading private sector efforts are Bridges to Excellence and the Leapfrog group. The former provides financial rewards to physicians who meet specified, evidence-based care standards for diabetes and heart conditions, and for using information technology in care delivery. The Leapfrog group focuses on rewarding improved patient safety in hospitals through public reporting.

There is no consensus about which strategies are most effective. Evidence of their impact on quality and costs varies widely by targeted conditions and types of interventions. Medicare demonstrations to provide case management to beneficiaries with catastrophic illnesses and high medical costs failed to improve client self-care or reduce Medicare spending in the early 1990s.

In contrast, an intervention to help elderly patients with congestive heart failure manage their care after hospital discharge has been shown to reduce hospital readmissions. Intensive programs to support diabetics' adherence to treatment regimens in the private sector can be effective in avoiding or delaying the onset of complications, although findings on cost savings are unclear.

Disease management and case management programs may allow Medicare to improve chronic care without increasing costs.

Despite these mixed results, a recent comprehensive review of care coordination programs concluded that care coordination has the potential to reduce utilization while maintaining or improving quality within the existing health system, and suggested that there are effective ways to coordinate care. Because high-cost beneficiaries with chronic conditions have many expensive hospital stays, strategies to improve care coordination and self-management for this group have the greatest potential. Disease management and case management programs may allow Medicare to improve chronic care without increasing costs.

Compared to the commercially insured, Medicare beneficiaries have more complex conditions, are more likely to be poor, frail, and cognitively impaired. Medicare's strength is that beneficiaries remain in Medicare once enrolled, so the program benefits from both short-term and long-term improvements in health and efficiency. These factors affect the design of strategies, and make it difficult to translate private-sector efforts and findings to Medicare. The Centers for Medicare and Medicaid Services (CMS) has begun testing a number of strategies.

The Medicare Prescription Drug, Improvement and Modernization Act of 2003

The Medicare Prescription Drug, Improvement and Modernization Act (MMA, P.L. 108-173) includes several provisions to test mechanisms designed to improve quality of care and reduce costs for chronically ill beneficiaries. Most initiatives are required to be budget neutral.

The *chronic care improvement program* (CCIP) aims to improve care and save money by providing ongoing care coordination across providers, using care management plans, teaching participants self-care techniques, and promoting the use of evidence-based treatment guidelines for fee-for-service beneficiaries with congestive heart failure, complex diabetes, or chronic obstructive pulmonary disease. Enrollee participation is voluntary. Contracts have been awarded for nine pilot projects for a three year period beginning December 2004. The fee paid to the contractor is contingent upon meeting quality, satisfaction, and savings targets. Contractors are required to save the program a minimum of 5 percent of health care costs, net of the program fees. If performance targets are met, CMS can expand the program to other areas without congressional authorization.

The *pay-for-performance demonstration* provides incentives to physicians to improve care management for fee-for-service beneficiaries with one or more selected chronic conditions. The aim is to stabilize medical conditions, limit acute episodes that result in expensive hospitalizations, and reduce adverse outcomes, such as drug interactions. Physicians who meet performance standards receive a fixed payment for each member. The three-year demonstration will operate in four sites.

The *capitated disease management demonstration* pays organizations a fixed sum per beneficiary in return for providing disease or case management services and all Medicare-covered benefits to beneficiaries with select chronic illnesses, such as stroke, congestive heart failure, or diabetes, and to frail elders or beneficiaries with Medicare and Medicaid coverage.

Other MMA provisions affecting chronic care:

- require sponsors of the Part D prescription drug plans to establish drug therapy management programs for members with multiple chronic conditions,

- direct the Secretary of Health and Human Services to develop a plan to improve care for the chronically ill,

- require a demonstration of hospice care in rural areas where none exist, and

- authorize the Institute of Medicine to evaluate performance measures

Other Programs

The *Medicare disease management demonstration* tests whether disease management services combined with prescription drug benefits improves care and saves money for fee-for-service beneficiaries with advanced-stage congestive heart failure, diabetes, or coronary artery disease. Enrollment in demonstration sites began in February 2004. The *physician group practice demonstration* is designed to encourage care coordination, promote efficiency through investment in administrative structure and process, and to reward physicians for improving health outcomes. Eleven group practices are expected to participate. These two demonstrations were mandated by the Medicare, Medicaid and SCHIP [State Children's Health Insurance Program] Benefits Improvement & Protection Act of 2000 (BIPA; P.L. 106-554).

The *coordinated care demonstration* tests the impact of various care coordination approaches—including both case and disease management—on quality and expenditures in the fee-for-service program. Fifteen programs targeting frail, elderly, and chronically ill Medicare beneficiaries operate in both urban and rural settings. This demonstration was mandated in the Balanced Budget Act of 1997 (P.L. 105-33). The *intensive case management demonstration* in Albuquerque, New Mexico (2001–2004) tests whether case management for high risk individuals with congestive heart failure and diabetes improves clinical outcomes, quality of life, and satisfaction. The *end stage renal disease* (ESRD) *disease management demonstration* tests the ability to improve quality of care in the fee-for-service program, traditional managed care plans, and special health plans that use interdisciplinary care teams. It was authorized by OBRA [Omnibus Budget Reconciliation Act] 1993 (P.L. 90-248); the sites have not yet been awarded.

CMS has also proposed to extend efforts by Medicare's quality improvement organizations (QIOs) to address the care of patients with multiple conditions. Beginning in August 2005, QIOs may be required to assist physician offices in providing chronic care for congestive heart failure, hypertension, depression, and coronary artery disease, and also to help physician offices adopt electronic prescribing to reduce misuse of prescription drugs.

CMS demonstration programs target conditions that are most likely to show short-term effects and savings. They also are designed to explore how to identify and target beneficiaries; identify and implement interventions that improve health and lower costs; and reward effective and efficient care. Challenges include integrating findings from these trials, avoiding duplication of effort across demonstrations, and determining how success will be measured. In addition, these demonstrations do not directly address the issue of how to share information among providers and programs (both within Medicare and with other insurers) to support coordinated care while still protecting beneficiaries' privacy.

An aging population, the addition of a prescription drug benefit, and federal budget deficits require policymakers to continue to explore ways to improve Medicare. Medicare's size makes it possible to consider and test options for improvement that smaller programs cannot.

Medicaid Eligibility Requirements Must Be Reformed

Stephen A. Moses

Stephen A. Moses is president of the Center for Long-Term Care Reform, an organization that promotes private payment for long-term care. He has been a Medicaid state representative for the Health Care Financing Administration and senior analyst for the inspector general of the U.S. Department of Health and Human Services.

Medicaid expenditures today exceed the cost of Medicare and continue to skyrocket. Medicaid is the biggest item in state budgets, having topped elementary and secondary education combined for the first time in 2004. Long-term care (LTC) accounts for one-third to one-half of total Medicaid expenditures in most states, 35 percent on average. For 2003, total Medicaid expenditures were $267 billion. Of this, Medicaid-financed nursing home care accounted for approximately $51 billion and home care $9.9 billion.

Medicaid LTC recipients consume a disproportionate share of total program expenditures. Consider, for example, people who are eligible for both Medicaid and Medicare. Such "dual eligibles" account for 42 percent of Medicaid spending, although they make up only 16 percent of Medicaid recipients. Dual eligibles are heavy users of LTC and Medicaid-financed acute care services that are not covered by Medicare. On top of this, Medicaid pays for Medicare premiums and cost sharing for dual eligibles.

Aged, blind, and disabled (ABD) individuals—also heavy users of LTC—make up one-fourth of Medicaid recipients but account for two-thirds of program costs, whereas poor women and children make up three-quarters of the recipients but account for only one-third of Medicaid expenditures. Clearly, there is an imbalance between the types of people who use Medicaid and the resources spent on them.

LTC is Medicaid's most expensive benefit. The heaviest users of LTC—those who are eligible for both Medicaid and Medicare and those who are aged, blind, or disabled—consume a disproportionate share of Medicaid's total resources. Therefore, every actual or potential dual eligible, ABD, or other LTC recipient who is kept from becoming dependent on Medicaid will result in disproportionate savings to the program. In other words, if policymakers can prevent Medicaid dependence for even a small number of these heavy LTC users, the savings would be extraordinarily high.

> There is an imbalance between the types of people who use Medicaid and the resources spent on them.

But aren't dual eligibles, the aged, blind, and disabled, and heavy LTC users the poorest of the poor? Isn't Medicaid their only safety net after a catastrophic spend-down has devastated their life's savings and driven them into financial destitution? Actually, the truth is not that simple. By confronting the true complexity of Medicaid eligibility, we can find the savings, fix the program, and improve LTC for everyone.

Are people on Medicaid necessarily poor? Only if they're young and need acute or preventive medical care. But not if their eligibility is based on their being aged, blind, or disabled and in need of LTC. Medicaid's financial eligibility rules are relatively tight for poor women and children. For people over the age of 65 who have a medical need for nursing-home-level care, however, Medicaid's eligibility rules—contrary to conventional wisdom—are very loose.

Income Eligibility

Even substantial income is rarely an obstacle to Medicaid eligibility for the elderly who require LTC. If they have too little income to pay all their medical expenses, including nursing home care, they're eligible. Medicaid "income eligibility" is determined in one of two ways. According to the Social Security Administration, 35 states and the District of Columbia have "medically needy" income eligibility systems. Those states deduct each Medicaid applicant's medical expenses—including private nursing home costs, insurance premiums, medical expenses not covered by Medicare, and so forth—from the applicant's income. If the applicant has too little income to pay for all of these expenses, he or she is eligible for Medicaid—not just for LTC but for the full array of Medicaid's optional services, which often stretch far beyond what Medicare covers.

The remaining states have "income cap" Medicaid eligibility systems. In those states, anyone with income of $1,737 or less per month (300 percent of the SSI monthly benefit of $579) is eligible for LTC benefits. But any additional income makes the applicant ineligible for Medicaid, even though that amount is not enough to pay privately for nursing home care. Thus, Congress approved "Miller income diversion trusts" in the Omnibus Budget Reconciliation Act of 1993 (OBRA '93). These special financial instruments allow people to siphon excess income into a trust to become eligible for Medicaid. The trust proceeds must then be used to offset the Medicaid recipient's cost of care, and any balance in the trust at death is supposed to revert to Medicaid. Nevertheless, Miller income trusts allow people with incomes substantially over the ostensible limit to qualify for Medicaid, take advantage of the program's low reimbursement rates, and receive an extensive range of additional medical services.

No one has to be poor to qualify for Medicaid. There is no set limit on how much income you can have and still qualify as long as your private medical expenses are high enough or, if you live in an "income cap" state, you have a Miller income diversion trust. All anyone needs to qualify for Medicaid is a cash-flow problem—that is, too little income after all medical expenses are deducted.

Asset Eligibility

One might ask, "So what?" Everyone knows that people must spend down their assets before becoming eligible for Medicaid. Here again the truth belies the conventional wisdom. Medicaid beneficiaries can easily retain unlimited assets while qualifying for Medicaid LTC benefits, as long as those assets are held in an exempt form. For example, Medicaid exempts one home and all contiguous property regardless of value. A simple "intent to return" to the home keeps it exempt, whether or not anyone resides in the home or the Medicaid applicant has any objective medical possibility of ever returning. How is this rule used to protect assets? . . .

Medicaid also allows an exemption for one business, including the capital and cash flow of unlimited value. . . .

Death and Divorce

A prepaid burial space is another excluded resource, regardless of value. This includes improvements or additions to such spaces as well as contracts for care. Medicaid eligibility workers often suggest prepaying burial expenses to expedite Medicaid eligibility.

Whole life and other kinds of life insurance that build equity are limited to a cash-surrender value (i.e., the amount that the policy holder can collect by voluntarily terminating the policy) of $1,500. But one can hold unlimited term life insurance with no effect on eligibility. Because the proceeds of a life insurance policy pass to beneficiaries outside a probated estate, not only can a term life policy shelter large assets from

Medicaid eligibility limits, it can also be used to avoid estate recovery.

Home furnishings are officially excluded regardless of value. Personal property that is held for "its value or as an investment" is a "countable resource." However, such assets are not usually counted, because Medicaid eligibility workers rarely verify whether such property is held for the purpose of investment or hiding assets. In fact, Medicaid eligibility workers often suggest that applicants purchase new or additional household goods to minimize the amount they have to spend down and expedite Medicaid eligibility.

There is no limit *to how much wealth people can stash . . . to become eligible for Medicaid.*

One car of unlimited value is exempt, assuming it is used to transport the Medicaid recipient or a member of the recipient's household. And because it is exempt, giving it away is not a transfer of assets to qualify for Medicaid, so the applicant can give one car away, buy another, give it away, and so on until he or she reaches the $2,000 eligibility threshold for nonexempt assets. That's called the "two Mercedes" rule. . . .

In spite of these generous special exclusions and exemptions, married couples are frequently advised to consider qualifying for Medicaid by getting a divorce. [As attorneys Hal and Debora Fliegelman put it:]

> Divorce is one of the more extreme Medicaid planning strategies. A successful divorce, in which both parties are represented by independent counsel, and containing an agreement in which most or all of the couple's assets are given to the community spouse, can result in almost immediate Medicaid eligibility for an institutionalized spouse.

[Attorney Michael Farley further states:]

> The divorce option will likely become increasingly attractive to the current generation of wealthy baby-boomers as they

near retirement age. They can hardly be expected to willingly give up the standard of living to which they have grown accustomed just because their spouse has suffered a catastrophic injury or illness that requires full-time medical care in a nursing home. It is unlikely that the current generation will feel it is beneath them to preserve their hard-earned assets by taking advantage of poorly drafted Medicaid legislation.

Bottom line, *there is no limit* to how much wealth people can stash in exempt assets or jettison by means of a calculated divorce settlement to become eligible for Medicaid LTC subsidies.

Medicaid Estate Planning

On top of these already generous income and asset limits, professional Medicaid planners—including attorneys, financial planners, accountants, and some insurance agents—use other techniques to protect additional hundreds of thousands of dollars for more affluent clients and their heirs. Such techniques include gifting strategies, annuities, trusts, life-care contracts, and dozens of others delineated in hundreds of books, law journal articles, and the popular media. The proceedings of the annual symposia and institutes of the National Academy of Elder Law Attorneys are a rich repository of the creative and highly profitable methods of Medicaid planning.

Hundreds of articles, legal treatises, and books spanning the past three decades are readily available in any law library. I have personally published over 100 columns describing the practice and techniques of Medicaid planning. To obtain even more references, one can simply conduct an Internet search for "Medicaid planning" and find more than two million links to sources, methods, and purveyors of artificial self-impoverishment techniques. Similar techniques allow people with substantial income and assets to avoid Medicaid's ostensibly mandatory estate recovery rules, although states rarely enforce these rules effectively. . . .

Medicaid Spend-Down

If Medicaid eligibility rules are so generous, why do so many Americans spend down into impoverishment before they become eligible for benefits? The answer is, they don't. Dozens of so-called "Medicaid spend-down" studies were conducted in the late 1980s and early 1990s that showed that spend-down was much less common than previously believed. Before those studies, academics assumed that one-half to three-quarters of all people in nursing homes had been admitted as private-pay patients and spent down until their life savings were consumed. Since the spend-down studies, however, we have known that the actual figure is less than one-quarter of nursing home residents who begin as private-pay patients and later convert to Medicaid. And, because none of those spend-down studies distinguished between people who spent down the conventional-wisdom way (writing big checks to a nursing home every month) and people who spent down the Medicaid planning way (writing one check to an elder law attorney), we have every reason to believe that genuine catastrophic spend down of real personal assets is even less than those studies indicated.

Out-of-Pocket Spending

If there is no reason to spend down assets, then why is such a large proportion of LTC spending composed of out-of-pocket expenditures? Again, the answer is, it isn't. Because Medicaid patients have to contribute their Social Security income toward their cost of care, the percentage of nursing home costs paid out of pocket is really much less significant than it appears. The Centers for Medicare and Medicaid Services (CMS) reports that out-of-pocket spending accounted for 27.9 percent of nursing home care spending in 2003 (down from 38.5 percent 15 years earlier). Nearly half of those out-of-pocket expenditures are actually the recipients' Social Security income, which the recipients are required to contribute to the cost of their care under Medicaid. That is to say, what is usually assumed to be spend-down of life savings is largely just money transferred from one government program (Social Security) to another government program (Medicaid). Back out the other major sources of nursing home financing as well (Medicaid at 46.1 percent in 2003, Medicare at 12.4 percent, private health insurance at 7.6 percent, and other public and private funds and State Children's Health Insurance Program at 6 percent), and one is left with only one dollar out of seven (14 percent) spent for nursing home care that could even possibly be coming from people's life savings. Fully 86 percent of all nursing home expenditures come from direct government funding (Medicaid and Medicare) plus indirect government funding (spend-through of Social Security income by people already on Medicaid) plus private health insurance, and much of the remainder comes from personal income other than Social Security (i.e., not from assets). There simply is no evidence of widespread catastrophic spend-down of personal assets for LTC.

The single most effective step . . . to fix Medicaid . . . would be to replace Medicaid's wide-open home equity exemption.

Medicaid is not primarily an LTC safety net for people who have spent down into impoverishment. Rather, it is the principal payor of LTC for nearly everyone regardless of economic status. Medicaid provides fewer than half the dollars expended for nursing home care but covers two-thirds of nursing home residents. And because Medicaid residents have the longest stays, the program touches more than 80 percent of all nursing home patient days. Home care is no different. Only 17 percent of home health care costs were paid out of pocket in 2003. The remainder comes from Medicaid, Medicare, and private health insurance.

The fundamental problem with LTC financing is that government pays for so much of it that the public has been anesthetized to the risk and expense of high-cost extended care. People can ignore the risk, avoid the premiums for private insurance, wait to see if they will need LTC, and transfer the cost to taxpayers. Is it any wonder that so few Americans buy private insurance or use reverse mortgages (see below) to finance LTC? Is it any wonder that most Americans who need LTC end up dependent on Medicaid? . . .

Medicaid is supposed to be America's LTC safety net for the poor. Instead, it is the principal LTC payor for nearly everyone. Medicaid's LTC benefit has become "inheritance insurance" for baby boomers, lulling them into a false sense of security regarding their own future LTC needs. Medicaid's loose eligibility rules for LTC create perverse incentives that invite abuse and discourage responsible LTC planning. The conventional wisdom that most people must spend down their life savings before they qualify for Medicaid LTC benefits is a myth.

If people's biggest asset, their home equity, were at risk to pay for LTC, most people would plan early to save, invest, and insure against that risk. Reverse mortgages permit people to withdraw supplemental income or assets from their otherwise illiquid home equity without risking use of the home. This extra cash can purchase services to help them remain at home and delay Medicaid dependence—or avoid it altogether. The single most effective step Congress and the president can take to fix Medicaid, reduce its cost, and improve the quality of LTC would be to replace Medicaid's wide-open home equity exemption with a more limited exemption of home equity or none at all.

With that one change in effect, families would pull together to fund quality LTC for their elders, rather than fighting over the spoils of Medicaid-planning abuse as they do now. That simple measure combined with other, lesser modifications would pump desperately needed oxygen into LTC markets, ease the tax burden of Medicaid, enable Medicaid to provide better access to higher-quality care for the genuinely needy, and supercharge the market for LTC insurance and home equity conversion products. Everyone will be better off, with the exception of legal experts who currently profiteer on Medicaid's extravagantly loose eligibility rules.

Ageism Prevents the Elderly from Getting Proper Medical Care

Alice Dembner

Alice Dembner is a staff writer for the Boston Globe *daily newspaper in Massachusetts.*

Older patients often suffer needlessly from cancer, depression, and heart disease because society's age bias gets in the way of treatment, according to a growing body of research.

Patients over 65 typically get less aggressive treatment for cancer than younger patients, less preventive care for high blood pressure and cholesterol, and double the dose they need of some psychiatric medicines, studies show.

While they represent the majority of patients with chronic illnesses and the major users of prescription drugs, they are frequently passed over for tests of new treatments and medicines, leaving doctors with little of the evidence they need to care for seniors properly.

"There is a persistent bias ... that works against the best interests of older Americans," said Daniel Perry, executive director of the Alliance for Aging Research, a nonprofit based in Washington that advocates for improvements in the health of aging Americans.

Doctors and advocates are struggling to chip away at the ageism, which they said often springs from misguided attempts to protect seniors from being harmed by overly aggressive treatments. In the latest volley, published [in February 2005] in the *Journal of the American Medical Association*, University of Vermont researchers showed that aggressive chemotherapy reduced deaths from breast cancer and recurrences in women over 65 as much as in younger women. Age alone should not rule doctors' and patients' decisions about cancer treatment, the researchers said.

Earlier studies of breast cancer treatment showed that many older women are not getting standard treatment, including life-saving chemotherapy. In fact, one study found that women over 65 with breast cancer that hadn't spread, and whose tumors didn't respond to antiestrogen therapy, were seven times less likely than younger women to get chemotherapy.

An Age Bias

The researchers, from Ohio State University, controlled for factors such as the size of tumors and stage of cancer, and concluded that age bias was a major factor.

The problem is not limited to women. About half of all seniors with advanced colon cancer don't get chemotherapy after surgery to remove the tumor, although older patients who get the treatment live longer, according to researchers at Columbia University.

---

*One study found that women over 65 with breast cancer
... were seven times less likely than younger women to
get chemotherapy.*

"Many older patients are not getting the optimal therapy for their cancer," said Dr. Edward Trimble, who heads efforts at the National Cancer Institute to improve cancer care for the elderly. "Bias is part of it."

Other factors, he said, are real concerns about the ability of frail seniors or those with multiple illnesses to tolerate aggressive treatments. But those decisions should be made on a case-by-case basis in consultation with the patient, he and other doctors said, and not decided based on myths about what an "average" old person can tolerate.

"Many physicians who take care of older people have not gotten the message that your chronological age is not your biological age," said Dr. Tamara Harris, a senior investigator at the National Institute on Aging. "Physicians need to take into account that being 65 doesn't mean you're close to the end of your life."

Seniors' own internalized ageism also contributes to undertreatment, doctors said. Older patients sometimes dismiss health problems such as hearing loss, memory problems, or incontinence as symptoms of old age and don't even mention them during office visits.

Doctors are plagued by some of those same misconceptions, according to other research. In a survey published in the *Journals of Gerontology,* 35 percent of doctors erroneously considered an increase in blood pressure a normal process of aging.

"We've seen a dramatic underuse of cholesterol drugs, even blood pressure drugs, in older people," said Dr. Jerry Avorn, a professor of medicine at Harvard Medical School who studies use of drugs. "The older you are, the more likely you are to have a chronic condition untreated with drugs."

A Mistaken Belief That Depression Is Normal

A report by the Alliance for Aging Research found a particular problem in psychiatric care, suggesting that "too many physicians and psychologists believe that late-stage depression and suicidal statements are normal and acceptable in older patients."

The suicide rate among older Americans is four times the national average, and 39 percent of older adults who commit suicide had been seen by their primary care physician in the previous week, according to the Alliance.

Many older patients also don't get screening and treatments to prevent disease. The federal Centers for Disease Control and Prevention reported in 2004 that six in 10 older adults hadn't gotten all recommended preventive services, including screening for common cancers and vaccines for flu and pneumonia. Seniors don't regularly get bone density tests either, although the tests can help assess risk for osteoporosis and fractures.

In some cases, the problem is at the other extreme: seniors are overmedicated because doctors don't know the optimal dose. Many drugs have not been studied extensively in the elderly, who typically metabolize drugs differently from younger people.

Physicians need to take into account that being 65 doesn't mean you're close to the end of your life.

The US Food and Drug Administration recommends, but does not require, drugs to be tested in the elderly.

A study of schizophrenia drugs in late 2003 found that seniors did well on about half the dose given to younger patients. The problem of overdosing is compounded, Avorn said, because some doctors dismiss symptoms of drug side effects, such as confusion or tiredness, as signs of aging.

The Elderly Are Excluded from Drug Trials

Seniors have often been excluded from tests of new treatments for many of the illnesses that are most common among those over 65. For example, the Vermont doctors who analyzed research on breast cancer found that only 8 percent of the 6,487 women in four large studies were over 65, despite the fact that about 50 percent of all new breast cancer cases are diagnosed in older women.

"A lot of older people are shortchanged," said Dr. Hyman Muss, a professor of medicine at the Vermont Cancer Center at the University of Vermont College of Medicine.

The Food and Drug Administration, in fact, found that seniors represented about 36 percent of patients in clinical trials for six of the most deadly cancers, despite the fact that seniors account for 60 percent of the cases of cancer of the breast, lung, colon, pancreas, ovaries, and blood.

The gap is largely due to the failure of physicians to ask seniors to participate, according to a study by New York researchers. In addition, some seniors are excluded because of complicating illnesses, while others choose not to participate.

This contributes to a vicious cycle, Avorn noted. "They get kept out of the studies and then people deny them the drugs because there's no evidence they work in the elderly," he said.

Change has begun, however.

The National Institute on Aging and the National Cancer Institute are spending millions of dollars on studies of disease and treatments in seniors.

Doctors' organizations are inviting Muss and other researchers who study age bias to speak about their results.

Ageism in healthcare is still an underrecognized problem.

Medical schools are incorporating more teaching about geriatric care into the curriculum. Medicare is paying for more preventive care, and beginning to pay doctors on the basis of the quality of care provided to seniors.

But Perry, of the Alliance, suggests that the biggest push for equality in care will come as the baby boomers turn 65 in the next few years.

"Ageism in healthcare is still an underrecognized problem," he said. "Reform will only come when the consumers of healthcare start demanding that their health needs are met with some urgency."

Elderly Minorities Receive Inferior Health Care

Kim Krisberg

Kim Krisberg writes about public health issues for Nation's Health, *the official newspaper of the American Public Health Association.*

Health disparities are a pervasive part of America's health care system, having been documented across the spectrum, from access to insurance to disease rates. Such disparities don't fade with age, which is why cultural competencies will be key in preparing for an older population more diverse than ever.

According to the U.S. Administration on Aging [AoA], the number of minorities ages 65 and older is expected to increase by 217 percent in the coming decades, compared with 81 percent for older whites. Specifically, black elders will increase by 128 percent, Asian elders by 301 percent, Hispanic elders by 322 percent and American Indian and Alaska Native elders by 193 percent. Unfortunately, many of the same disparities and barriers that plague younger minorities will continue into old age, when health care can be even more vital to a person's quality of life.

Older minorities tend to be in poorer health than the general population, have more functional impairments, more limited educations and lower incomes, and in turn, bear more out-of-pocket costs. Such costs average about 19 percent of total income for all Medicare beneficiaries, AoA reported, but about 28 percent for those in poorer health, 21 percent for those without a high school diploma and more than 31 percent for those at the lowest income levels. Besides economic challenges, many older minorities face language and transportation barriers and report more negative encounters with health care providers. Nonetheless, early research shows that "culturally competent" health care can change how older—and younger—minorities interact with the health care system by building on community traditions and respecting cultural beliefs. For public health workers in particular, cultural competency will be key if their life-saving prevention methods are to be accessible to all older Americans.

However, to have a lasting impact on health disparities in old age, efforts must be made to reach younger generations as well, according to Peggye Dilworth-Anderson, PhD, director of the Center for Aging and Diversity at the Institute on Aging at the University of North Carolina at Chapel Hill.

"You have these social determinants that have an effect over a life course, like education, discrimination, tenuous job situations, problematic access to the economic structure . . . it's a bigger issue than access to care," Dilworth-Anderson [said]. "When I see many older minority people, they're the ones that have survived."

Health Workers Must Understand Culture

It is important when working across diverse populations to understand the values and histories of a culture, as many older minorities have experienced "horrendous social injustice, many forms of discrimination and adversity," Dilworth-Anderson said. Learning a community's history will help health workers understand why some are reluctant to participate in health research and highlight the importance of first developing relationships with key leaders in a community, she said. And health workers should be wary of "over-romanticizing" the fact that minority elders are more likely to live with their families, she noted.

"There is an upside (to taking in elders), but there's also a downside in terms of the burdens and the risks of taking on that level of dependency and we need to develop more support for those families," she said. "When families do this ... they're adhering to many strong cultural values and beliefs, but the cost side of that is that families often have limited resources themselves ... so families are often weakened by absorbing the needs of elders."

However, public health workers can take advantage of larger households by engaging an older person's immediate support network in the promotion of good health, said Clayton Fong, executive director of the National Asian Pacific Center on Aging. Living with elderly family members is often an issue of necessity for Asian families, Fong said, as many Asian communities are located in expensive urban areas. And although within Asian culture there is "more of a tendency to support and honor elders, one could make the case that's becoming less and less ... the longer we've been here, the weaker that likelihood," he said.

Older minorities tend to be in poorer health than the general population, ... and in turn, bear more out-of-pocket [health] costs.

Older Asian populations bear higher incidences of certain cancers coupled with higher mortality and morbidity rates, but unfortunately there is very little definitive research on the health of Asian elders. Often, the gap is created by omitting the number-one cultural competency needed for working with older Asians: language. If a research project has no language capability, a researcher simply won't get a representative sample of an Asian community, Fong said. Plus, in a lot of data at the federal level, Asian subpopulations aren't broken out, even though different groups experience different disease rates. For example, Pacific Islanders have higher heart disease and diabetes rates, while Japanese people have a lower heart disease rate, he noted.

"For older Asian Americans, the most critical need is language," Fong [said]. "About 60 percent of Asian Pacific elders don't speak English well and one-third have no one in the house that speaks English. . . . (For health workers), finding bilingual staff will be key."

In fact, once appropriate language skills are employed to reach older Asians, the response is overwhelming. Recently, the National Asian Pacific Center on Aging set up three toll-free helplines in Cantonese and Mandarin, Korean and Vietnamese, and since October [2004], the lines have received about 10,000 calls nationwide, Fong said. He attributes part of the response to the helplines being established around the same time as changes to the nation's Medicare program were initiated. Even so, after Asian-language newspapers began writing about the helplines, "calls would literally back up the voicemail line and as fast as we could download messages, it would get filled up again," Fong said.

"For a lot of folks who don't have the access, when you do break the barrier down, the needs are huge and the response is gigantic," he said.

Language Remains a Key Barrier

Among the changes stemming from the Medicare Prescription Drug, Improvement and Modernization Act of 2003—which was enacted in December 2003—was a benefit to help low-income seniors purchase prescription drugs. In their outreach to help low-income Asian seniors take advantage of the benefit, Fong and his colleagues found that when left to fill out the paperwork on their own, 90 percent could not do it correctly. What made the difference was having access to a multilingual helpline, according to Fong.

"The good news is once we started doing this, we found that folks were not only eligible for the benefit, but we found substantial people eligible for Medicaid that had not signed up," he said.

Fong emphasized that choosing how and through which vein to communicate with a minority population is the key between success and failure.

"To health workers: Take advantage of the media—there's a large Asian-language media out there," he said. "A lot of times our government-funded health hasn't figured that niche out. We're still in that one-size-fits-all mode."

Knowing the language and culture is also critical for the success of health activities among older Hispanic people, said Yanira Cruz, MPH, president and chief executive officer of the National Hispanic Council on Aging. Learning how to communicate with the Hispanic population could help curb diseases such as diabetes, which affects about one in three elderly Hispanics, and lower cancer-related mortality rates by urging Hispanics to get screened early, according to Cruz.

Many of the same disparities and barriers that plague younger minorities will continue into old age.

"Clearly, a lot of these conditions have an important health education and promotion element that is often missing in the Hispanic community because we don't have enough providers that understand people's language, culture and belief system," Cruz told *The Nation's Health*. "Having a poor relationship with a health care provider makes it very difficult for an elderly Hispanic person to be able to take full advantage of the body of science . . . and to be able to incorporate it into their lives."

Similar to the National Asian Pacific Center on Aging, when Cruz and her colleagues began educating older Hispanic communities on the new Medicare prescription drug benefits, they found a huge gap in information.

"We are very concerned that our (Hispanic) elderly are not aware of this program and so they will be missing out on this opportunity and, in fact, may be hurt by not taking action," Cruz said. . . .

"The health care system is very complex and for a population that traditionally has achieved little education status, it's hard to understand new programs," she said. "To that complexity, you add information targeted through electronic means and problems become even bigger because for the Hispanic population, the digital divide is huge."

Finances Can Be a Barrier

Financial issues in general are a big problem for older Hispanics, Cruz said, adding that "having to choose between a meal and medications—it is common to see that." Health care providers need to be aware of such hardships when working with an older Hispanic patient. For example, prescribing a lower cost generic medication instead of a brand-name helps ensure a patient can sustain a regimen, Cruz noted.

To effectively bring health promotion and prevention programs to elderly Hispanic communities, health workers should partner with already trusted community-based organizations, she said. Also, Spanish-language radio, television and newspapers are major mechanisms of reaching older Hispanics.

"It's critical that we get messages of prevention and health promotion to our communities and specifically to have a targeted effort to the Hispanic elderly," Cruz said. "It's a growing population, and if we don't prevent some of the serious complications, our health care system will suffer tremendously due to expenses managing these complications."

The key to getting the message out is going where the audience goes, according to Angie Boddie, director of health programs at the National Caucus and Center on Black Aged Inc., which has been serving black and low-income elders for 35 years. Health promotion campaigns need to tap into urban markets, utilize mass transportation, target "mom-and-pop" shops, barber shops, beauty salons—"go where minorities go,"

Boddie said. A main venue for reaching elderly blacks with prevention messages is through churches, she said.

"By far, working with pastors is incredible," Boddie told *The Nation's Health.* "If you can get a pastor on your side, you've pretty much struck gold."

Boddie also conducted educational outreach on the new Medicare drug benefit, and similarly found that the Internet presented a major barrier to enrollment. In computer labs at housing sites owned or operated by the National Caucus and Center on Black Aged Inc., Boddie and colleagues organized events to help seniors enroll online, finding that "expecting them to do it on their own was an absolute no-go."

The number of minorities ages 65 and older is expected to increase by 217 percent in the coming decades, compared with 81 percent for older whites.

"Literacy is a very big deal even though you may speak English," she said. "You never know what education level a group has, so you have to be very sensitive and really find a balance to addressing your audience."

In collaboration with officials at the Centers for Medicare and Medicaid Services [CMS], Boddie is working to ensure Medicare materials are culturally sensitive. For example, many older black women use hand fans, so CMS created hand fans with Medicare information printed on them. Boddie also serves many Korean elders and is working with CMS to offer Medicare presentations in Korean.

However, most of the inquiries Boddie receives are about Alzheimer's disease, which is more prevalent among blacks than whites, according to the Alzheimer's Association, which described the disease among blacks as a "silent epidemic." However, because of "ethnic and cultural bias" in screening and assessment tools, blacks have a much higher rate of false-positive results and also tend to be diagnosed in later stages of the disease, the association reported.

"(Alzheimer's) is becoming okay to talk about now and families want information," Boddie said. "I can't cure the world but if I can reach people with information, I can empower them."

Earning Trust Is Key to Successful Outreach

In some minority populations, earning trust among the elder generation could mean gaining trust among the entire community. In American Indian and Alaska Native communities, elders are often the main stakeholders, "so if health systems want more involvement, elders can be very influential to encourage trusting systems and utilizing them," according to Candace Fleming, PhD, director of training with the American Indian and Alaska Native Program at the University of Colorado Health Sciences Center.

"Minority populations are living longer and we need elders to be a vital part of our communities," Fleming said. "Especially for Indian communities, where elders are the carriers of cultural information."

Most Indian elders are not insured, receiving services through the federal Indian Health Service [IHS]. The system is "wonderful in many areas," Fleming said, but typically IHS doesn't have many geriatric specialists available and there's usually not enough funding to adequately address elder needs. Also, many American Indian and Alaska Native elders don't have retirement plans and although they're many times eligible for federal aging programs, they often don't have the assistance they need to get enrolled, Fleming noted. However, being able to reach American Indian and Alaska Native elders with prevention messages, especially around diabetes—which is epidemic in some Indian communities—could help bridge access gaps.

"Many successful programs are rooted in grassroots belief systems around the honored place of elders," Fleming [said]. "Also, there's work to develop innovative strategies to get out prevention and promotion using natural gatherings."

Choosing how and through which vein to communicate with a minority [elderly] population is the key between success and failure.

Natural gatherings are traditional times during the year that American Indians and Alaska Natives gather together, Fleming said. So, in addition to attending health fairs and visiting elder housing areas, health workers are also attending natural gatherings to spread promotion and prevention messages. Besides population-based outreach, working one-on-one with an American Indian or Alaska Native elder also requires that a provider be sensitive to cultural ideas about illness and healing.

"Elders have a whole host of avenues for self-care based on belief systems that are more than just European medicines," Fleming said. "So, a provider has to listen carefully to what the elder is saying with regards to the meaning of symptoms, ideas for healing and ideas for intervention."

Above all, Fleming said, health workers should involve American Indian and Alaska Native communities in the development of elder health programs and work through already trusted channels.

"Work through the tribal government structure to identify the elder-serving part of that organization and get its buy-in into the effort," she said.

Rural Americans Lack Health Access

Being culturally competent not only comes into play when working with older minorities, but with rural elders as well. For older rural Americans, the biggest issue is access to appropriate care, according to R. Turner Goins, PhD, associate director for research at the Center on Aging at West Virginia University. In rural areas, there's less of everything except for nursing home beds, Goins said, adding that even though home and community-based services are less expensive than nursing homes, such services are hard to develop in rural areas.

"The thrust is to keep older adults in the community as long as possible . . . but there's not a lot of alternatives except for the nursing homes for older (rural) adults," she [said]. "They prematurely get placed in nursing homes before they need to be because there's no other supportive services."

Rural areas often suffer from health care provider shortages, with only about 10 percent of physicians practicing in rural America, despite the fact that one-fourth of the nation's population lives in rural communities, according to the National Rural Health Association. To help alleviate the shortage, many international medical graduates serve in rural, underserved areas as part of their requirements to practice in the United States. However, there hasn't been much research into how well such providers work with older rural adults or how well they acclimate into their surroundings, Goins noted.

"What we've heard from older adults in West Virginia, is that these physicians have done a wonderful job integrating into the community," she said. "But in other communities, there have been cultural barriers. It's an interesting phenomenon."

One way of overcoming such barriers is to learn local colloquialisms. For example, Goins said, in a 2001 study in rural West Virginia, one participant said he felt "riggoty." Goins said she automatically thought he meant tired, but upon further probing, she found he meant full of energy and pep.

"It's important to use a cultural interpreter in these situations," she said. "If an older patient wants to bring in a daughter-in-law or spouse, (the provider) should encourage that."

Overall, Goins' message is similar to other advocates': Involving community gatekeepers in health outreach is critical to a program's success. For public health workers, in particular, cultural competencies will be crucial in helping all Americans live longer, healthier lives.

"Public health workers have the training, have the compassion, have the desire to engage in this type of intervention," said Cruz of the National Hispanic Council on Aging. "With a little help from the academic centers and schools of public health, our practitioners will become even more effective in working with emerging communities."

The Alzheimer's Epidemic Threatens to Overwhelm the Health Care System

Salynn Boyles

Salynn Boyles, a freelance reporter for WebMD, has been writing about medical issues for more than a decade.

The number of Americans with Alzheimer's disease will triple over the next 50 years unless new ways to prevent or treat the degenerative condition are found, according to newly revised national figures.

Thirteen million elderly people in the U.S. are projected to have the disease in the year 2050, compared to about 4.5 million (in 2003).

The Health-Care Crisis of the Century

The larger-than-expected increase could easily overwhelm the nation's health-care system within the next few decades. Alzheimer's Association president Sheldon Goldberg tells WebMD that the approaching epidemic represents, "the health-care crisis of the century." The advocacy group co-funded the study along with the National Institute of Aging (NIA).

"If left unchecked, it is no exaggeration to say that Alzheimer's disease will destroy the health-care system and bankrupt Medicare and Medicaid," Goldberg said in a news release.

The upward revision is largely due to improved survival among the very elderly—those who are 85 years and older. Advances in the treatment of heart disease, cancer, and other diseases associated with aging mean that people are living longer than ever.

Within 30 years, Alzheimer's cases among this age group are projected to double, and cases will quadruple within 50 years unless something changes, lead researcher Denis A. Evans, MD, of Chicago's Rush-Presbyterian-St. Luke's Medical Center tells WebMD.

The larger-than-expected increase [in Alzheimer's victims] could easily overwhelm the nation's health-care system within the next few decades.

Using Alzheimer's figures derived from 3,900 elderly Chicagoans, Evans and colleagues projected the number of Americans with Alzheimer's disease will increase from roughly 4.5 million to 5.7 million within the next 20 years. Within four decades, estimates are that 11 million people will have Alzheimer's, and within five decades, 13.2 million. The findings are reported in the August (2003) issue of the journal *Archives of Neurology*.

An Increase over Earlier Projections

The 2050 estimate represents a 35% increase over projections for the same time period reported by Evans and colleagues [in 1990]. Evans says better methods of measuring survival increases among the elderly led to the new figures.

If the Alzheimer's projections and U.S. Census Bureau future population figures turn out to be accurate, then one in 26 Americans will have Alzheimer's disease in the year 2050, compared to roughly one in 64 [in 2003].

That is a depressing thought, but one that NIA Alzheimer's expert Marcelle Morrison-Bogorad, PhD, says is not likely to happen if the commitment to Alzheimer's research remains strong. The federal government will spend roughly $640 million this year [2003] to study the disease, but the Alzheimer's Association is calling for a funding increase to $1 billion annually.

Research to Delay Disease

Morrison-Bogorad, who is associate director for the NIA's Neuroscience and Neuropsychology of Aging Program, says she is optimistic that research will lead to ways to delay Alzheimer's onset. That, in turn, could have a profound impact on its overall incidence. Because Alzheimer's disease primarily afflicts the very old, NIA research suggests that delaying disease onset by five years could result in a 50% overall reduction in cases.

Within four decades, estimates are that 11 million people will have Alzheimer's, and within five decades, 13.2 million

---

"I don't think we are going to solve the mystery of Alzheimer's disease next year or within the next few years. The brain is very complicated and we don't really know much about how it works, even when it is healthy," Morrison-Bogorad tells WebMD. "But we already know much more than we did a decade ago."

She says studies like Evans' are important because they illustrate just how quickly the number of Alzheimer's disease cases will grow if the commitment to research lags.

"I am sure that with time we will have a much better idea of which one of the possible therapeutic approaches being studied out there will actually have a chance of success," she says.

CHAPTER 3

Should Social Security Be Privatized?

Chapter Preface

Social Security is a public pension plan administered by the federal government. President Franklin Delano Roosevelt created the Social Security system in 1935 as part of the New Deal, a series of programs designed to promote economic recovery and social reform during the Great Depression. Today, Social Security is the country's largest social program. More than two-thirds of older Americans rely on monthly Social Security checks as their main source of retirement income, and nearly 20 percent count on it as their only income.

Social Security was established as part of a public safety net to ensure the financial well-being of elderly people, but some analysts claim that the program faces a financial crisis. Unless changes are made, most experts agree that beginning in 2014, Social Security will have insufficient funds to pay retirees their full benefits. As aging baby boomers—the 76 million Americans born between 1946 and 1964—retire, these experts claim, the number of people who collect benefits will rise while the number of younger workers who contribute to the program will decline. Social Security is a "pay-as-you-go" system in which the benefits distributed to retirees currently collecting Social Security are paid for by taxes on the earnings of those who are still working. The Social Security debate is thus sometimes cast as a battle between senior citizens and younger generations over scarce resources. How best to prevent the eventual depletion of Social Security is controversial. One solution, which is the subject of rigorous debate, is to privatize Social Security—to transfer the responsibility for Social Security to private citizens.

President George W. Bush is a staunch advocate of privatizing Social Security. In May 2001 Bush created a bipartisan, sixteen-member commission to study the ailing Social Security system. He asked the commission to make recommendations about how best to modernize the system and solve its financial problems. The commission agreed that allowing workers to invest part of their Social Security money in personal retirement accounts would be the best way to keep the program healthy so that it could provide retirement benefits for future generations of seniors. Citizens could invest their Social Security money in the stock market, mutual funds, or bonds, for example. Supporters argue that privatizing Social Security would give individuals ownership of their futures and allow them to earn higher interest on their retirement money.

While Bush and other supporters tout privatization as a way to save Social Security, opponents claim that doomsday predictions about the future of the program are exaggerated. Drastic restructuring of the venerable program, they argue, is unnecessary. They believe that making smaller adjustments such as increasing the age at which benefits can be collected or reducing the monthly amount seniors receive is a better way to keep the program solvent.

Many seniors' organizations vigorously oppose efforts to privatize Social Security. Since the market is extremely unpredictable, opponents maintain, encouraging investment in the stock market is too risky. Critics maintain that privatization will not bring the expected payoffs and will therefore further erode the public safety net for the poorest seniors, actually increasing the risk of poverty among seniors who live increasingly longer lives. Women, they maintain, would be especially hard hit by such a policy change because they typically live longer than men and are more likely to rely on Social Security as their only source of income.

Whether privatizing Social Security is the best way to protect the retirement income of older Americans remains controversial. The authors in this chapter express their views on this contentious issue.

Privatizing Social Security Will Benefit All Americans

George W. Bush

George W. Bush is the forty-third president of the United States.

Editor's Note: President George W. Bush delivered this speech from the East Room of the White House on April 28, 2005.

Congress ... needs to address the challenges facing Social Security. I've traveled the country to talk with the American people. They understand that Social Security is headed for serious financial trouble, and they expect their leaders in Washington to address the problem.

Social Security worked fine during the last century, but the math has changed. A generation of baby boomers is getting ready to retire. I happen to be one of them. Today there are about 40 million retirees receiving benefits; by the time all the baby boomers have retired, there will be more than 72 million retirees drawing Social Security benefits. Baby boomers will be living longer and collecting benefits over longer retirements than previous generations. And Congress has ensured that their benefits will rise faster than the rate of inflation.

In other words, there's a lot of us getting ready to retire who will be living longer and receiving greater benefits than the previous generation. And to compound the problem, there are fewer people paying into the system. In 1950, there were 16 workers for every beneficiary; today there are 3.3 workers for every beneficiary; soon there will be two workers for every beneficiary.

Social Security Is Headed for Bankruptcy

These changes have put Social Security on the path to bankruptcy. When the baby boomers start retiring in [2008], Social

George W. Bush, televised press conference, Washington, DC, April 28, 2005.

Security will start heading toward the red. In 2017, the system will start paying out more in benefits than it collects in payroll taxes. Every year after that the shortfall will get worse, and by 2041, Social Security will be bankrupt.

Franklin Roosevelt did a wonderful thing when he created Social Security. The system has meant a lot for a lot of people. Social Security has provided a safety net that has provided dignity and peace of mind for millions of Americans in their retirement. Yet there's a hole in the safety net because Congresses have made promises [they] cannot keep. . . .

I believe a reform system should protect those who depend on Social Security the most.

As we fix Social Security, some things won't change: Seniors and people with disabilities will get their checks; all Americans born before 1950 will receive the full benefits.

Our duty to save Social Security begins with making the system permanently solvent, but our duty does not end there. We also have a responsibility to improve Social Security, by directing extra help to those most in need and by making it a better deal for younger workers. Now, as Congress begins work on legislation, we must be guided by three goals. First, millions of Americans depend on Social Security checks as a primary source of retirement income, so we must keep this promise to future retirees, as well. As a matter of fairness, I propose that future generations receive benefits equal to or greater than the benefits today's seniors get.

Secondly, I believe a reform system should protect those who depend on Social Security the most. So I propose a Social Security system in the future where benefits for low-income workers will grow faster than benefits for people who are better off. By providing more generous benefits for low-income retirees, we'll make this commitment: If you work hard and pay into Social Security your entire life, you will not retire into poverty. This reform would solve most of the funding challenges facing Social Security. A variety of options are available to solve the rest of the problem, and I will work with Congress on any good-faith proposal that does not raise the payroll tax rate or harm our economy. I know we can find a solution to the financial problems of Social Security that is sensible, permanent, and fair.

Reforms Replace Promises with Results

Third, any reform of Social Security must replace the empty promises being made to younger workers with real assets, real money. I believe the best way to achieve this goal is to give younger workers the option, the opportunity if they so choose, of putting a portion of their payroll taxes into a voluntary personal retirement account. Because this money is saved and invested, younger workers would have the opportunity to receive a higher rate of return on their money than the current Social Security system can provide.

We have a shared responsibility to fix Social Security and make the system better.

The money from a voluntary personal retirement account would supplement the check one receives from Social Security. In a reformed Social Security system, voluntary personal retirement accounts would offer workers a number of investment options that are simple and easy to understand. I know some Americans have reservations about investing in the stock market, so I propose that one investment option consist entirely of Treasury bonds, which are backed by the full faith and credit of the United States government.

Options like this will make voluntary personal retirement accounts a safer investment that will allow an American to build a nest egg that he or she can pass on to whomever he or she chooses. Americans who would choose not to save in a personal account would still be able to count on a Social Security check equal to or higher than the benefits of today's seniors. . . .

I will work with both the House and the Senate as they take the next steps in the legislative process. I'm willing to listen to any good idea from either party.

Too often, the temptation in Washington is to look at a major issue only in terms of whether it gives one political party an advantage over the other. Social Security is too important for "politics as usual." We have a shared responsibility to fix Social Security and make the system better; to keep seniors out of poverty and expand ownership for people of every background. And when we do, Republicans and Democrats will be able to stand together and take credit for doing what is right for our children and our grandchildren.

Privatizing Social Security Gives Workers Control Over Their Future

Michael Tanner

Michael Tanner is Director of Health and Welfare Studies for the Cato Institute, a libertarian research organization.

For the past several years there has been a growing consensus about the need to reform Social Security. As the debate has developed, the Cato Institute has provided studies and other information on the problems facing Social Security and the advantages of individual accounts as a way to reform the system. But until now we have not suggested a specific plan for reform.

Now, however, the debate has advanced to the point where it becomes important to move beyond generalities and provide specific proposals for transforming Social Security to a system of individual accounts. The Cato Project on Social Security Choice, therefore, has developed a proposal to give workers ownership of and control over their retirement funds.

This plan would establish voluntary personal accounts for workers born on or after January 1, 1950. Workers would have the option of (a) depositing their half of the current payroll tax (6.2 percentage points) in an individual account and forgoing future accrual of Social Security retirement benefits or (b) remaining in the traditional Social Security system and receiving the level of retirement benefits payable on a sustainable basis given current revenue and expenditure projections.

Workers choosing the individual account option would have a variety of investment options, with the number of options increasing as the size of their accounts increased. The initial default option would be a balanced fund, weighted 60 percent stocks and 40 percent bonds. Workers choosing the individual account option would also receive bonds recognizing their past contributions to Social Security.

At retirement, workers would be able to choose an annuity, a programmed withdrawal option, or the combination of an annuity and a lump-sum payment. The government would maintain a safety net to insure that no senior would retire with income less than 120 percent of the poverty level.

We expect this proposal to restore Social Security to long-term and sustainable solvency and to do so at a cost less than the cost of simply continuing the existing program. And it would do far more than that.

Workers who chose the individual account option could accumulate retirement resources substantially greater than those that are currently payable under traditional Social Security. They would own and control those assets. At the same time, women and minorities would be treated fairly, and low-income workers could accumulate real wealth.

Most important, this proposal would reduce Americans' reliance on government and give individuals greater responsibility for and control over their own lives. It would provide a profound and significant increase in individual liberty.

The Social Security Crisis

Social Security as we know it is facing irresistible demographic and fiscal pressures that threaten the future retirement benefits of today's young workers. Although Social Security is currently running a surplus, according to the system's own trustees, that surplus will turn into a deficit within the next 15 years. That is, by 2018 Social Security will be paying out more in benefits than it takes in through taxes.

In theory, Social Security is supposed to continue paying benefits after 2018 by drawing on the Social Security Trust Fund. The trust fund is supposed to provide sufficient funds to continue paying full benefits until 2042, after which it will be exhausted. At that point, by law, Social Security benefits will have to be cut by approximately 27 percent.

However, in reality, the Social Security Trust Fund is not an asset that can be used to pay benefits. Any Social Security surpluses accumulated to date have been spent, leaving a trust fund that consists only of government bonds (IOUs) that will eventually have to be repaid by taxpayers. . . .

Even if Congress can find a way to redeem the bonds, the trust fund surplus will be completely exhausted by 2042. At that point, Social Security will have to rely solely on revenue from the payroll tax—but that revenue will not be sufficient to pay all promised benefits. Overall, Social Security faces un-funded liabilities of nearly $26 trillion. Clearly, Social Security is not sustainable in its current form. . . .

Social Security taxes are already so high, relative to ben-efits, that Social Security has quite simply become a bad deal for younger workers, providing a low, below-market rate of return. That return has been steadily declining and is expected to be less than 2 percent for most of today's workers.

The poor rate of return means that many young workers' retirement benefits will be far lower than if they were able to invest their payroll taxes privately. On the other hand, a sys-tem of individual accounts, based on private capital invest-ment, would provide most workers with significantly higher returns. Those higher returns would translate into higher re-tirement benefits, leading to a more secure retirement for mil-lions of seniors.

Savings and Economic Growth

Social Security operates on a pay-as-you-go (PAYGO) basis; almost all of the funds coming in are immediately paid out to current beneficiaries. This system displaces private, fully funded alternatives under which the funds coming in would be saved and invested for the future benefits of today's workers. The result is a large net loss of national savings, which reduces capital investment, wages, national income, and economic growth. Moreover, by increasing the cost of hiring workers, the payroll tax substantially reduces wages, employment, and economic growth.

Shifting to a private system, with hundreds of billions of dollars invested in individual accounts each year, would likely produce a large net increase in national savings, depending on how the government financed the transition. That would increase rational investment, productivity, wages, jobs, and economic growth. Replacing the payroll tax with private retirement contributions would also improve economic growth because the required contributions would be lower and would be seen as part of a worker's direct compensation, stimulating more employment and output.

Social Security is not sustainable in its current form.

In 1997 Harvard economist Martin Feldstein estimated that, if all Social Security payroll taxes were privately invested, that investment would produce a net benefit of from $10 trillion to $20 trillion in present value. That is his estimate of the present value of the improved economic performance that would result from the reform. Most of that net benefit would probably come in the form of higher returns and benefits earned for retirees through the private investment accounts. But some would also come in the form of higher wages and employment for working people.

Helping the Poor and Minorities

Low-income workers would be among the biggest winners under a system of privately invested individual accounts. Private investment would pay low-income workers significantly higher benefits than can be paid by Social Security. And that does not take into account the fact that blacks, other minorities, and the poor have below-average life expectancies. As a result, they tend to live fewer years in retirement and collect less in Social Security benefits than do whites. Under a system of individual accounts, by contrast, they would retain control over the funds paid in and could pay themselves higher benefits over their fewer retirement years, or leave more to their children or other heirs.

The higher returns and benefits of a private investment system would be most important to low-income families, as they most need the extra funds. The funds saved in individual retirement accounts, which could be left to the children of the poor, would also greatly help families break out of the cycle of poverty. Similarly, the improved economic growth, higher wages, and increased jobs that would result from an investment-based Social Security system would be most important to the poor. Moreover, without reform, low-income workers will be hurt the most by the higher taxes or reduced benefits that will be necessary if we continue on our current course. Averting a financial crisis and its inevitable results would consequently be most important to low-income workers.

In addition, with average- and low-wage workers accumulating huge sums in their own investment accounts, the distribution of wealth throughout society would become far broader than it is today. That would occur not through the redistribution of existing wealth but through the creation of new wealth, far more equally held. Because a system of individual accounts would turn every worker into a stockowner, the old division between labor and capital would be eroded. Every laborer would become a capitalist.

Ownership and Control

After all the economic analysis, however, perhaps the single most important reason for transforming Social Security into a system of individual accounts is that it would give American workers true ownership of and control over their retirement benefits.

Many Americans believe that Social Security is an "earned right." That is, they think that, because they have paid Social Security taxes, they are entitled to receive Social Security benefits. The government encourages this belief by referring to Social Security taxes as "contributions," as in the Federal Insurance Contributions Act (FICA). However, the U.S. Supreme Court has ruled, in the case of *Flemming v. Nestor*, that workers have no legally binding contractual or property right to their Social Security benefits, and those benefits can be changed, cut, or even taken away at any time.

As the Court stated, "To engraft upon Social Security a concept of 'accrued property rights' would deprive it of the flexibility and boldness in adjustment to ever changing conditions which it demands." That decision built on a previous case, *Helvering v. Davis*, in which the Court had ruled that Social Security is not a contributory insurance program, stating that "the proceeds of both the employer and employee taxes are to be paid into the Treasury like any other internal revenue generally, and are not earmarked in any way."

In effect, Social Security turns older Americans into supplicants, dependent on the political process for their retirement benefits. If they work hard, play by the rules, and pay Social Security taxes their entire working lives, they earn the privilege of going hat in hand to the government and hoping that politicians decide to give them some money for retirement.

In contrast, under a system of individual accounts, workers would have full property rights in their private accounts. They would own their accounts and the money in them the same way they own their individual retirement accounts (IRAs) or 401(k) plans. Their retirement benefits would not depend on the whims of politicians.

Privatizing Social Security Will Benefit the Economy

David Malpass

David Malpass is chief economist for Bear Stearns, a worldwide investment banking, securities trading, and brokerage company.

It's tempting to call Social Security reform dead and move on. That's what I read in the newspapers every day. But the idea underlying it is too good, pro-growth, and saleable to drop.

The current Social Security system is an unfunded liability, meaning there are no investments to back up future payments. The benefits of reforming the system would be immense for the U.S. economy and financial markets. Reform would partially fund retirement benefits with real investments, put workers' names on their accounts, pave the way to full funding, relieve the growing generational strains from a pay-as-you-go system (FDR [Franklin D. Roosevelt] himself said it should only last for a limited period), add to economic growth and jobs, and correct some of the income- and health-related unfairness in the current system.

> *The benefits of reforming the system would be immense for the U.S. economy and financial markets.*

Unfortunately, the sales job has let Social Security reform sound scary to the elderly, complex to the young, and, perhaps worst of all, too radical to many voters. A sound reform will be the opposite—about as radical and risky as IRAs [individual retirement accounts], but with big positive impacts on economic growth and jobs.

Here are eight compelling reasons to reform Social Security now:

1. We must begin funding the Social Security commitment. The current system is an unfunded liability in which Social Security taxes fund current outlays. There isn't any investment associated with the taxes. Opponents of Social Security reform have no plan, nada, to fund the future payments or allow workers to invest their Social Security taxes. The private sector doesn't promise future benefits without funding them, and the government shouldn't.

2. Social Security reform will mean less dependence on Washington. Retirees now rely on Washington's largesse for their checks. There's no contract. The size of the trust fund could be raised or lowered or zeroed out through legislation, making it clear that the trust fund is simply a figment of Washington's financial imagination. Retirees pay lobbying associations millions in dues to increase the odds that their checks will continue and grow. Workers will be under Washington's thumb for life, first paying tax rates set in Washington, then hoping for big checks. Our democracy would function better if we got a statement showing our retirement savings free and clear of Washington. For now, every election has to be first a vote on the size of Social Security payments, then a vote on other issues.

Privatization Would Spur the U.S. Economy

3. Social Security reform, because it is structural in nature, would be a major pro-growth change in the operation of the U.S. economy, breaking the U.S. out of one of the entitlement boxes, a reform that increasingly characterizes mature democracies. Structural reforms are the holy grail of market-based economic development, the rare time in history when a country materially improves its long-term economic prospects. The U.S. shouldn't pass up this opportunity. The message it will send to ourselves and the world is invaluable: that we can ma-

terially improve our fiscal condition by relying on ownership more than on the federal government.

4. Jobs! When you tax something less, you get more of it, in this case jobs. The current Social Security system imposes a gigantic tax on jobs—12.4 percent of pre-tax income including the employer and employee portions. Washington happily spends all the proceeds and asks for more. Reducing the tax wedge by allowing workers to invest it would cause more jobs and a higher average U.S. growth rate, a key yet unspoken selling point for Social Security reform.

5. Fairness. How politicians can be proud of the current system is beyond me. It is unfair to those, whether the frail or minorities, who tend to die earlier and lose their benefits. It's unfair to those who want to work past 62 or start working young, since the benefit formulas (unlike a personal account) give minimal extra benefit for working more years. And it's unfair to those with earnings less than the $90,000 earnings cap, because they bear the full brunt of the high tax payments going into Washington's fiscal black hole. Increasing the earnings cap would just extend the unfairness to more workers. The problem isn't the earnings cap. It is the high tax rate for an unfunded liability that discourages work, penalizes early death, and pays a low return.

Privatization Would Reduce Risks

6. Less risk, more benefits. In today's system, the government spends all the payroll taxes and decides the formulas for paying benefits. This creates an immense risk to the young—that a future government will want to spend less on them. The oddity in the current debate is that it compares the notional benefit formula in a shaky, completely unfunded system to private sector returns and somehow concludes that the latter is more risky. At most, the current benefit system offers an assumed return of 3 percent per year, but that is completely dependent on the beneficiary living long enough to collect, Washington enacting a huge tax increase to pay the benefits

when the trust fund runs out, and then deciding to protect full Social Security payments from other government programs like Medicare. In a February 28 [2005] *Wall Street Journal* article, Jeremy Siegel, one of the world's experts on long-term equity performance, is quoted forecasting real equity returns (before inflation) at 6 percent per year over the next 44 years, with bonds expected to yield substantially less. Personal accounts clearly offer the likelihood of more benefits than the current system, without the risk of the government voting them away.

7. Fiscal soundness, better benefit structure. One important reason to reform Social Security is to improve the benefit formulas. Under the current system, Social Security outlays will soon grow to 130 percent of Social Security receipts. The growth aspects of Social Security reform would narrow this gap. A reform process also offers a unique opportunity to change the benefit structure, perhaps by indexing initial benefits to inflation rather than wage rates, and adding benefits for lower income workers.

8. Big step to tax reform. Social Security reform is arguably more important than tax reform, but that's saying a lot. It's vital for growth that Washington spend time legislating new tax rules. The best route is to complete a solid Social Security reform and then clear the congressional deck for tax battles. Otherwise, current law will force millions into higher tax rates, increase the cost of capital, and undo many of the economic and job gains of recent years.

In sum, *Social Security reform should be selling itself.* It benefits the elderly by recommitting the country to their existing payments and improving the system for their children and grandchildren. It benefits the middle-aged by letting them own part of their retirement savings, while improving the country's growth, jobs, stock market, and fiscal outlook. And it benefits the young by giving them concrete ownership in a growing part of their retirement savings.

Private Social Security Accounts Should Not Replace Guaranteed Benefits

Jeffrey B. Liebman

Jeffrey B. Liebman is a professor of public policy at the Kennedy School of Government at Harvard University. From 1998 to 1999 he served as special assistant to President Bill Clinton for economic policy.

The current discussion of ways to reform the U.S. Social Security retirement system is becoming increasingly polarized over the issue of "privatization." This divide unfortunately obscures the fact that the views of most Democrats and Republicans on the subject are not that far apart: a bipartisan solution should be achievable. More important, by lumping together all reforms that involve personal retirement accounts (PRAs), this polarization obscures critical differences between PRA-based plans that *raise* future standards of living and preserve the social-insurance features of the current system, and those that have few or no economic benefits to offset their high administrative costs, added risk, and reduced redistribution from rich to poor. Given that a PRA-based plan may well be enacted ..., it is critical that the public understand that all such plans are not created equal.

Aging Americans, Anemic Savings

Retirement policy in the United States faces two challenges. The first is the long-term imbalance of the Social Security system. Although the system is currently running surpluses, the aging of the population implies that in about a dozen years expenditures will outstrip revenues. By 2050—around the time [the 2005] Harvard seniors reach retirement—scheduled benefits are projected to exceed revenues by 35 percent and the gap will continue to grow thereafter.

We should keep the magnitude of this shortfall in perspective. In 2050, the system will bring in enough revenue to pay 73 percent of scheduled benefits—and would support benefits that are larger in inflation-adjusted terms than the benefits received by today's retirees. So the perception that Social Security will not be there at all for today's younger workers is a myth.

Moreover, the projected shortfall in 2050 is only 1.7 percent of projected gross domestic product (GDP). This is dwarfed by Medicare's long-run financial gap, and by the current shortfall of 5 percent of GDP in the federal budget excluding Social Security and Medicare. Indeed, simply returning the tax code to what it was when President Clinton left office would produce more than enough extra revenue to cover the entire Social Security shortfall. The irony is that the non–Social Security fiscal imbalances have become so large that reforming Social Security—previously the untouchable third rail of American politics—has become attractive in comparison.

The perception that Social Security will not be there at all for today's younger workers is a myth.

The second retirement-policy challenge is that too few Americans have significant savings to supplement their income from Social Security. Social Security is designed to provide a solid foundation for financial well-being in retirement, *not* to cover a retiree's entire income needs. Private pensions and savings are meant to provide the rest. Unfortunately, for too many older Americans, Social Security is essentially all there is: one-third receive 90 percent or more of their income from Social Security and almost two-thirds receive more than half their income from the program. Thus, an important goal for retirement policy should be to encourage all workers to accumulate sufficient individual savings so the combination of Social Security and private nest egg allows them to maintain their standard of living during retirement. Proposals to introduce personal retirement accounts as part of Social Security can be seen as an attempt to deal with this second challenge.

Here is where the potential for a bipartisan solution comes in. Almost every reform plan, Democratic and Republican, includes some combination of benefit cuts and additional revenue to bring the traditional system into balance. And most Democrats and most Republicans support proposals to encourage savings on top of the traditional Social Security benefit. The substantive differences between the two parties' proposals involve the balance between tax increases and benefit cuts used to bring the traditional Social Security system into balance, and the extent to which the savings incentives are described as part of Social Security or as a separate program. Democratic reform plans tend to maintain higher benefit levels and therefore to rely more heavily on tax increases to restore the traditional system. And Democratic plans generally try to maintain a distance between savings incentives and Social Security. Republican plans rely more heavily on benefit cuts or on the hope that stock market gains will make tax increases and benefits cuts unnecessary, and these plans generally divert payroll tax revenue directly into PRAs. But these are not fundamentally different approaches; they are the kinds of differences that can be bridged in a legislative compromise.

The Political Debate

Why then is the debate over personal retirement accounts so contentious? Political grandstanding, of course, plays a role. But there is a substantive reason as well. People who place a high value on the social-insurance features of the current system worry that once the Pandora's box of personal retirement accounts is opened, it will be hard to control what will come out. Thus, even if it is possible in theory to design a PRA-based plan that preserves the best features of the current Social Security system while simultaneously increasing private savings, there is no guarantee that this is what the political process will yield.

The reason it is hard to predict what will happen is that three different groups support personal retirement accounts with three different goals in mind.

The first group sees PRAs as a politically feasible and economically efficient way to set aside additional resources to meet future retirement needs. This group believes that replacement rates (the ratio of retirement income to pre-retirement income) should be maintained or increased and that current generations should sacrifice some consumption to raise the standard of living of future generations. People in this group tend to support using new tax revenues on top of the existing 12.4 percent Old-Age, Survivors, and Disability Insurance (OASDI) payroll tax to fund personal retirement accounts.

Social Security is designed to provide a solid foundation for financial well-being in retirement, not *to cover a retiree's entire income needs.*

The second group sees PRAs as a politically feasible way to cut Social Security benefits so as to limit the share of the nation's resources consumed by the elderly. This group believes that, given the aging of the population, replacement rates should fall—that the economic costs of maintaining a system as generous as the current one are too high. Thus this group believes we should try to come as close as possible to living within the current 12.4 percent payroll tax. The typical plan from people in this group funds personal retirement accounts by diverting a portion of the payroll tax to PRAs.

The third group believes that Social Security was basically a mistake in the first place—that it is not the government's job to provide for retirement, beyond perhaps a minimal welfare program. For this group, the mixed plans under consideration are the first steps toward total privatization.

The Bush administration appears to be dominated by people in the last two groups. Moreover, in promoting the virtues of PRAs, the Bush administration has not been forthcoming about the benefit cuts and revenue demands of its approach. Instead, it has emphasized features like "choice," voluntary participation, "ownership," and inheritability—features that make Social Security reform appear painless and that are directly at odds with the social-insurance aspects of the current program. In this charged environment, many strong supporters of social insurance have become unwilling to advance their own PRA-based proposals for Social Security reform; instead, they have adopted the tactic of opposing all plans that include personal retirement accounts.

The Economic Effects of Personal Retirement Accounts

In addition to the risks of opening Pandora's box, there is also considerable uncertainty about the economic effects of any given PRA-based reform plan. PRAs have the potential to provide two main economic benefits. First, they can increase national savings, thereby raising future standards of living. Second, they can increase the perceived link between people's OASDI tax payments and their ultimate retirement income, thereby encouraging labor supply by motivating individuals to work longer, or more. But it is far from certain that a PRA-based plan will have these effects.

If PRAs are designed so as to reduce current consumption—by requiring people to make contributions above the current 12.4 percent payroll tax to fund the accounts—the direct effect of the plan will be to raise national savings. But if the PRAs are funded by diverting some share of existing payroll tax revenue and increasing the deficit—as President Bush is apparently about to propose—then the reform will have, at best, no direct effect on national savings, and may even reduce savings

Reform plans can have large *indirect* effects on savings as well. If Congress raises other taxes or cuts other spending in response to the increase in the deficit created by Social Security reform, even a plan like President Bush's could raise national savings. Recent news accounts suggest, however, that the administration is trying to come up with new budgetary rules that would hide the increase in the deficit created by Social Security reform. If true, then the Bush-style plan is unlikely to raise national saving through this indirect channel, either.

The combination of Social Security and private nest egg allows [the elderly] to maintain their standard of living during retirement.

It is also possible that Social Security reform will affect the saving decisions of individual workers, but it is very hard to predict whether the net result will be to increase or decrease saving. Individuals might react to legislated reductions in Social Security's replacement rates by increasing their savings, hoping to ensure that they still have enough resources for retirement. Or they might believe that Social Security reform has increased the chance that they *will* receive significant benefits in retirement and therefore decide that they no longer need to save as much on their own. Individuals might learn the benefits of saving from watching their PRA balances grow and start making additional contributions to 401ks and IRAs [individual retirement accounts]. Or they might decide that because they have PRAs they no longer need to contribute to IRAs and 401ks, and net personal savings could decline.

The magnitude of the economic gains from increasing the perceived link between OASDI tax payments and ultimate retirement income is similarly uncertain. While PRA plans have the potential to make people feel that their OASDI contributions are going directly into their own accounts and are therefore not a tax, many such plans—including the main plan of President Bush's 2001 Social Security commission—are so complicated that they could conceivably reduce the extent to which people perceive a connection between what they pay in and what they get out of the system.

Moreover, the potential economic benefits from PRAs can, in theory, be accomplished without such accounts. To increase national savings, we could simply raise taxes or cut spending. To increase the perceived link between Social Security taxes and benefits we could adopt a national accounts system like those in Sweden or Italy, in which the basic pay-as-you-go structure is preserved, but the relationship between a person's contributions and retirement benefits is transparent. In other words, the main value of PRAs is as a mechanism to achieve economically desirable policies that would otherwise be politically infeasible to enact or sustain.

Privatizing with Protections Preserved

Given the uncertainties about what form a PRA-based Social Security reform plan will take and the economic impacts it would have, what should a strong supporter of social insurance do? One option is to reject personal retirement accounts and try to solve Social Security's problems with a combination of tax increases (for example, by repealing the cap on the level of earnings subject to the Social Security tax) and benefit cuts. After all, this has been the traditional approach to Social Security reform.

In my judgment there are two reasons to abandon the traditional approach and, instead, to embrace personal retirement accounts. The political reason is that in the current anti-tax environment, it is unlikely that significant tax increases are going to be enacted as part of Social Security reform. Therefore, the only feasible way to devote the extra resources to Social Security that will allow us to maintain replacement rates in the future is to do so via personal retirement accounts.

The economic reason is that we need to save the tax increases for Medicare and Medicaid. Over the next century, the share of national income that we will want to devote to healthcare will likely rise substantially and, because much of healthcare in the United States is paid for via the public sector, we will need to increase tax rates substantially to cover those costs. Although there is considerable debate about the magnitude of the economic costs of taxation, they are certainly not zero. We should therefore try to solve the Social Security problem with as little economic distortion as possible, relying on forced saving via PRAs and leaving the explicit tax increases to pay for future healthcare costs.

But is it possible to design a mixed system—combining scaled-back traditional benefits with personal retirement accounts—that preserves the best features of the current Social Security system? The answer is yes, provided the mixed system has the following six features.

Maintain replacement rates. The main function of Social Security is to prevent a large drop in living standards in retirement for people who, through bad luck or bad planning, do not reach retirement with sufficient savings. As wage levels rise over time, Social Security benefits therefore need to rise with wages. Otherwise, retirement standards of living would fall further and further behind those of the pre-retirement period.

The Bush administration is apparently going to propose moving from wage-indexing to price-indexing as a way to implement large benefit cuts in the traditional Social Security program. To pave the way for this proposal, the administration is trying to turn attention away from the concept of replacement rates and instead have people focus on real benefit levels. They are arguing that it is crazy for the financially insolvent Social Security system to provide real benefits in 2050 that are 40 percent higher than today's. But that argument misses the point of Social Security. Would we want today's seniors to have a 1950s standard of living?

There are, however, two serious arguments for letting replacement rates fall a bit over time—though not nearly as far as the administration seems likely to propose. As the population ages, the tax rates necessary to pay Social Security benefits will have to rise, raising the amount of economic distortion caused by financing the program. We may therefore want to have a Social Security system that provides a bit less protection, rather than incur all of the incremental economic costs of higher taxes. In addition, because income levels rise over time due to productivity growth, we may reasonably be a bit less worried about people suffering a drop in their standard of living at retirement—given that the amount of hardship caused by, say, a 40 percent drop in consumption is likely to be lower if the initial level of consumption is higher.

But these arguments assume that replacement rates are set optimally to begin with. As I mentioned earlier, we need to find a way to *raise* retirement-income levels for retirees who lack significant savings beyond Social Security. For the two-thirds or so of Social Security beneficiaries in this category, our goal for Social Security reform should be to have the sum of the traditional benefit and personal retirement accounts *increase* their replacement rates, not *reduce* them.

Avoiding Pitfalls

Maintain a substantial guaranteed benefit. In calculating the replacement rate provided by a reformed Social Security system, one needs to count both the income provided by the scaled-back traditional Social Security benefit and the income from the personal retirement accounts. These two components are not equivalent, however, because one provides a certain income stream free from market risk, while the amount of income from the other depends on how one's investments perform. Regardless of the overall replacement rate provided by the reformed system, it is important that a significant portion of the benefit remain free from market risk. Today, the replacement rate for a typical worker retiring at age 62 (the most common retirement age) is about 33 percent (a bit higher in after-tax terms). In a reformed system that combined a traditional benefit with PRAs, it would seem prudent to have the traditional benefit continue to provide an income-replacement rate of at least 20 percent with the PRA making up (or more than making up) the remainder. This is a very modest requirement: it would mean that for a worker who, through Social Security and private saving, manages to replace 80 percent of pre-retirement income—a goal often suggested by financial planners—the traditional Social Security benefit would be accounting for only one-fourth of the total.

Avoid the slippery slope. One of the main dangers of mixed Social Security systems that combine traditional benefits with PRAs is that they might become the first step toward total privatization. The scenario is easy to envision: this year, we divert 3 percent of the 12.4 percent payroll tax to personal retirement accounts, as proponents argue that this modest change preserves a strong traditional benefit. Then, assuming the stock market does well for the next couple of years, the 2008 Republican platform calls for diverting another 3 percent. Pretty soon, we have no traditional benefit left.

The way to avoid this risk is to establish a clear principle that none of the 12.4 percent payroll tax should *ever* be diverted to personal retirement accounts. Instead, the accounts should be funded with new resources above the 12.4 percent tax. In this scenario, there will still need to be significant cuts in traditional benefits—because in the long run a payroll tax rate of 12.4 percent can support only about 60 percent of currently scheduled benefits. So we end up with a scaled-back traditional system funded with the 12.4 percent payroll tax and personal retirement accounts funded with, for example, an additional 3 percent of payroll contribution. Such a system, with a total cost of 15.4 percent of payroll, would allow us to maintain total replacement rates above current levels, even if the stock market performs somewhat less well in the future than it did during the past century.

Another benefit of insisting that the PRAs be funded with new money is that it maximizes the chance that the reform raises national savings.

Protect investors from high costs and poor investment decisions during accumulation. Individuals can mismanage their retirement savings in two ways. The first is to invest in mutual funds with high expense ratios. Investing in a mutual fund with an expense ratio of 1.25 percent reduces one's retirement resources by about 20 percent compared with investing in a fund with an expense ratio of 0.25 percent. In theory, competition should produce low fees. But in practice mutual funds manage to compete on non-fee dimensions (glossy brochures, sales incentives for distributors), and the average equity mutual fund charges fees of 1.25 percent. Normally, it is not the government's role to prevent consumers from making bad choices: for example, we don't stop people from purchasing Advil at one and one-half times the price of generic ibuprofen. But in the case of Social Security, the government has an interest in preventing people from making stupid decisions because people who end up destitute in old age will become a public responsibility.

The second way in which people can mismanage their retirement saving is to invest in an inappropriate portfolio. Judging the appropriate portfolio for each individual is difficult because it is hard to observe an individual's tolerance for risk. Nonetheless, there is some evidence that the main danger is that people will be too cautious—say by investing only in bonds for their entire lives.

Small personal-retirement-account plans are unlikely to be cost effective.

The solution to these problems is to allow people to invest only in a limited number of large broad-based index funds with regulations on fees and the minimum and maximum fraction of the portfolio that can be invested in stocks. Note that even this mixed system would produce income-replacement rates of only about 40 percent, so people would still need to continue to do additional retirement saving in IRAs and 401ks. People who desire a different overall asset allocation than that of the Social Security PRAs could do so by altering their other portfolios.

Costs Must Be Minimized

Finally, the accounts themselves need to be structured to minimize administrative costs, which are essentially a fixed amount per account. The cost does not depend on the account balances because nearly all of the expense comes from mailing account information to consumers, processing requests for changes in addresses or investment allocations, and answering customer questions via the telephone—all factors independent of account balances. In addition, the typical PRA will have account balances that are smaller than those of the average mutual-fund investor today. So small personal-retirement-account plans are unlikely to be cost effective—a plan probably needs to have contributions that are at least 3 percent of payroll to be worthwhile. Accordingly, administrative costs need to be assessed as a fraction of portfolio balances, not on a per-account basis, lest the fees consume a disproportionate share of the return for low earners. And there will likely need to be limits on the services provided: statements mailed annually rather than quarterly, restrictions on how frequently investors can alter their investment allocation, and perhaps even a charge per telephone inquiry.

Protect retirees during decumulation. Even though much of the debate over personal retirement accounts has focused on methods for structuring investments during the phase of life when workers are accumulating assets in their accounts, it is the design of the "payout" that largely determines whether a reformed system delivers a level of retirement-income security similar to that in the current Social Security system. In the current system, retirement benefits are paid in the form of real annuities that are indexed for inflation, last as long as a beneficiary lives, and are free from financial-market risk. In contrast, the most prominent legislative proposals for PRAs pay little attention to the payout phase, and even plans that specify a payout design tend to follow the Federal Thrift Savings Plan in not mandating annuitization and not guaranteeing benefits for surviving spouses. To fully replicate the protective features of the current system, full annuitization into fixed real annuities must be required of all workers, married couples must use joint-and-survivor annuities, and the government probably needs to be the annuity provider in order to keep administrative costs low.

Maintain redistribution. Finally, the Social Security benefit formula is progressive, providing a higher level of retirement income relative to lifetime earnings for low earners than for high earners. Although low earners tend to have shorter life expectancies than high earners and therefore receive benefits for fewer years, they still receive higher benefits relative to contributions than higher earners do. In contrast, a PRA plan that made deposits equal to 3 percent of payroll into each worker's account would not redistribute from high earners to low earners. Many different mechanisms could be used to maintain the existing level of redistribution in a Social Security system that includes PRAs. One would be to make higher deposits (relative to earnings) into the accounts of low earners. Another would be to make the traditional benefit formula more redistributive to offset the lack of redistribution in the PRA portion of the system. (But fans of the traditional system tend to be wary of this second approach because they feel that making Social Security too redistributive undermines its broad-based support.)

Including Protections from the Start

Some people argue that we do not need to worry about all of the details of a PRA system at the time it is introduced. After all, they maintain, there will be plenty of time to figure out the details as account balances accumulate, because it will be decades before people have to depend on PRAs for a substantial share of their retirement income. Indeed, many of the most important features of the current Social Security system—survivor benefits, disability benefits, automatic cost-of-living adjustments—were introduced after the original 1935 Social Security Act.

The Social Security benefit formula is progressive, providing a higher level of retirement income relative to lifetime earnings for low earners than for high earners.

I believe that this argument is wrong. Although the protections in the current Social Security system were developed gradually over time, introducing those protections almost always involved politically popular benefit *expansions*. In contrast, in a defined-contribution PRA system, introducing protections over time will typically require *reductions* in expected retirement-income levels, and so will be perceived as the government taking money away from account holders. For example, requiring joint-and-survivor annuities to protect widows will reduce monthly payments compared to requiring single-life annuities. Similarly, introducing a requirement that a greater fraction of account balances be converted into an annuity upon retirement could be perceived by some as the government taking money away from them. Therefore, it is essential that these provisions be included in the PRA system from the start to ensure that a reformed system continues to provide the level of protection that Americans count on from Social Security.

Privatizing Social Security Would Create Too Much Personal Risk

Jacob S. Hacker

Jacob S. Hacker is an assistant professor of political science at Yale University and a fellow at the New America Foundation, a nonpartisan, nonprofit public policy institute.

In a 1938 address on the third anniversary of the Social Security Act, Franklin Roosevelt [FDR] declared, "There is still today a frontier that remains unconquered; an America unclaimed. This is the great, the nationwide frontier of insecurity, of human want and fear. This is the frontier, the America we have set ourselves to reclaim." And reclaim it FDR and his fellow thinkers did.

In the three decades after Roosevelt's words were spoken, the great "frontier of insecurity" shrank dramatically. A massively expanded Social Security program, the GI bill, disability insurance, Medicare and Medicaid all expressed a commitment to protect Americans against what Roosevelt had once called the "hazards and vicissitudes" of modern industrial life.

Corporate America also got into the act. Employers constructed vast structures of security from guaranteed private pensions to generous health and life insurance that shielded millions from uncertainty and fear.

If the debate over Social Security suggests anything, it is that today's "pioneers" are moving sharply in the other direction. Those government programs of shared insurance are under sustained, and sometimes successful, assault. Those elaborate corporate systems of social protection are in steady decline. The political consensus that once helped push back the boundaries of insecurity has come undone, leaving Americans exposed to the vagaries of a harsh 21st century capitalism.

Riding the Economic Roller Coaster

The evidence of this Great Risk Shift is everywhere. Some 1.5 million Americans file for bankruptcy each year, more than half because of medical causes. Levels of consumer debt are at an all-time high. In 2003, 45 million Americans lacked health insurance, up more than 5 million since 2000. Those lucky enough to have a pension plan at work are less likely to get a guaranteed benefit. Even the great engine of economic growth in the 1990s, the hot job market, has cooled.

Seemingly overnight, Americans are experiencing the roller-coaster ride of life on the other side of insecurity's frontier. The instability of families' incomes has increased dramatically over the last 20 years. The typical family doesn't rise steadily to greater heights on the economic ladder, but like a volatile stock, its income oscillates wildly from year to year. And when families fall, they fall farther and faster, and government and the private sector do less to slow their descent.

In a world of growing insecurity, we need insurance against catastrophic events more than ever.

The causes of the Great Risk Shift are complex and multiple. The popular answer is "globalization," which suggests a trend beyond human control. Another part is the changing family: the simultaneous movement of women into the workforce, and the growing fragility of traditional family structures. But what's crucial is that these forces don't preordain the new financial order with which Americans now cope. It's within the power of political and corporate leaders to help Americans deal with these new and newly intensified risks. Yet neither has stepped up. As a result, Americans' basic assessments, expectations, and values have been thrown into a blender of conflicting perceptions and ideals, from which only political turmoil has emerged.

Conflicting Expectations

After World War II, the expansion of economic security laid the groundwork for reigning assumptions about economic and family life. Companies provided relatively stable employment. Standards of living rose. Two-earner families were a luxury, not a necessity. And when disaster struck, government and the private sector were there to cushion the fall. Today, Americans' expectations are conflicted, as are the nation's fierce debates over how government and business should respond. You rise and fall on your own, the devil on one shoulder says. Why support institutions of common protection? We are all in this together, the angel on the other shoulder retorts. How can we not have such institutions?

The trends seem to point in both directions at once. In a world of growing insecurity, we need insurance against catastrophic events more than ever. And yet the experience of Americans screams out "you're on your own" more than ever.

Old assumptions are dying hard. But most Americans still remain stubbornly reluctant to embrace the tough-minded alternatives offered in their place as the public hostility to a Social Security overhaul vividly shows. Opinion surveys show levels of public concern about economic security that were not seen even during the bad old economic days of the late 1970s and early 1980s. Yet the same polls also show a complete and total lack of confidence in American political institutions and leaders to address this problem.

The Social Security fight is a metaphor for the entire nasty struggle. Defenders of Social Security point to the huge costs of a transition to private accounts, the benefit cuts that would be implied, the gamble that the stock market represents. Yet their defense is mostly about a program, not about a principle. It is about what government does and should continue to do, not about what government should stand for in an era of increasing economic insecurity. On the other side, the principles are clear and far-reaching. The call for reform is the call for personal responsibility, for the rugged individualism that FDR's rhetoric about insecurity placed squarely in the nation's past. It is the past made future; the old assumptions reborn, but this time in the fancy new mantle of the "ownership society."

Personal Risk Increases

Say this for advocates of fundamentally revamping American social protections: They know where they want to go. President Bush's message is that government should establish the basis for financial independence and then let the chips fall where they may. Ownership means personal responsibility. Ownership means personal reward. And ownership means personal risk.

Americans still remain stubbornly reluctant to embrace the tough-minded alternatives offered in [Social Security's] place.

Americans like the first part of the message. But they remain skeptical of the second half, that misfortune is almost always a personal rather than a social problem. Scratch the surface of public opinion on almost any contested issue surrounding economic risk from health insurance to unemployment protection to retirement security and you find a complex picture that defies easy ideological summary. Americans may be rugged individualists when it comes to upward mobility, but they are committed social reformers when it comes to downward economic loss.

The challenge for those who hope to stoke this lurking reformist spirit is to develop an agenda that threads between the uncritical embrace of the old and the thoughtless celebration of the new. President Bush was right when he said, in his convention speech, that Americans' most basic social protections were constructed for a previous era, when work and family were more stable and certain.

Reclaiming Security

And yet, the road map that Bush and his allies seem to pull from this reality that we should work to make Americans' economic lives even more unstable and uncertain is the opposite direction we need to head in. Adaptation to a tumultuous new world does not mean capitulation to its darkest manifestations. It means reclaiming a role and place for basic economic security in a world in which such security has become harder and harder to find.

The potential blueprints are many: universal savings accounts, expanded health insurance, a system of catastrophic income protection for American families. They will remain blueprints, however, until truth is spoken to power on one of the most pressing domestic challenges America faces. Perhaps then we can once again look back with satisfaction on FDR's prediction that economic insecurity is the last great frontier that "we have set ourselves to reclaim."

The Traditional Social Security Program Helps Americans Share Life's Risks and Rewards

Barack Obama

Barack Obama is a Democratic United States senator from Illinois.

Editor's Note: Barack Obama delivered the following speech to the National Press Club in Washington, D.C., on April 26, 2005.

Rather than focus simply on the usual back and forth of the debate, one of the things I want to do today is to think about some of the larger issues that are at stake in the Social Security debate that's taking place in this country.

I can't help thinking about the America that FDR [President Franklin Delano Roosevelt] saw when he looked out from the window of the White House from his wheelchair: an America where too many were ill-fed, ill-clothed, ill-housed and insecure; an America where more and more Americans were finding themselves on the losing end of the new economy and where there was nothing available to cushion their fall.

Some thought that our country didn't have a responsibility to do anything about these problems, that people would be better off left to their own devices and the whims of the market.

Others believed that American capitalism had failed and that it was time to try something else altogether.

But our president, FDR, believed deeply in the American idea. He understood that the freedom to pursue our own individual dreams is made possible by the promise that if fate causes us to stumble or fall, our larger American family will be there to lift us up; that if we're willing to share even a

Barack Obama, speech before the National Press Club, Washington, DC, April 26, 2005.

small amount of life's risks and rewards with each other, then we'll all have a chance to achieve our God-given potential.

And because Franklin Roosevelt had the courage to act on this idea, individual Americans were able to get back on their feet and build an unprecedented shared prosperity that's still the envy of the world.

The New Deal[1] gave laid-off workers a guarantee that he or she could count on unemployment insurance to put food on the table while they looked for a new job.

It gave the young man who suffered a debilitating accident assurance that he could count on disability benefits to get him through the tough times.

A widow might still be able to raise her children despite the loss of a spouse without the indignity of asking for charity.

And Franklin Roosevelt's greatest legacy promised the couple who put in a lifetime of sacrifice and hard work that they could retire [with] dignity and respect because of Social Security.

The Times Have Changed

Now, . . . we're told by those who want to privatize that how much things have changed since FDR's days justifies the proposals that they're making.

I couldn't agree more that things have changed drastically since FDR's time. A child born in this new century is likely to start his life with both parents or a single parent working full-time jobs. They'll try their hardest to juggle work and family but they'll end up needing child care to keep that child safe, cared for and educated.

They'll want to give him the best education possible. But unless they live in a wealthy town with good public schools

1. The New Deal was President Franklin D. Roosevelt's framework for stabilizing the U.S. economy during the Great Depression.

they'll have to settle for less or find the money for private schools.

That student, as he or she gets older, will study hard and dream of going to the best colleges in America. But with tuition rising higher and faster than ever before, 519 percent over the last 25 years, he or she may have to postpone those dreams or start life deeper in debt than any generation before them.

After a lifetime of hard work and contribution to this country, do we tell our seniors that they're on their own?

And when that student graduates from college, he or she will find a job market where middle-class manufacturing jobs with good benefits have long been replaced with low-wage, low-benefit service sector jobs and high-skill, high-wage jobs of the future.

To get those good jobs, this young man or young woman will need the skills and knowledge not only to compete with other workers in America, but with highly skilled and knowledgeable workers from all over the world who are being recruited by the same companies that once made their home in the United States of America.

And when this student, he or she, finally starts a job, he'll want health insurance. But rising costs mean that fewer employers can afford to provide the benefits. And when they do, fewer employees can afford the premiums, the co-payments and the deductibles.

When this young man or young woman starts a family, he or she will want to buy a house and a car and pay for child care and college for his or her own children. But as he or she watches the lucky few benefit from lucrative bonuses and tax shelters, he'll see that his own tax burden, when you combine the federal, state and local, is rising and his own paycheck is barely this month's bills.

And when he retires, he'll hope that he and his wife have saved enough. But if there wasn't enough to save for retirement, he'll hope that there will still be at least two Social Security checks that come to the house every month.

Insecurity Is Growing

Here's the point: There are challenges that we are facing in the 21st century that we shouldn't exaggerate. We're not seeing the absolute deprivations of the Great Depression. But it cannot be denied that families face more risk and greater insecurity than we have known for a very long time, even as those families have fewer resources available to pull themselves out of difficult situations.

Whereas people once were able to count on their employers to provide health care, pensions and a job that would last a lifetime, today's workers wonder if suffering a heart attack will cause his employer to drop his coverage. He has to worry about how much he can contribute to his own pension fund. And he fears the possibility that he might walk into work tomorrow and find his job outsourced.

Now, just as the naysayers in Roosevelt's day told us that there was nothing we could do to help people help themselves, people in power today are telling us that instead of sharing the risks of this new economy, we should make them shoulder those risks on their own.

In the end, that's what I think the debate over the future of Social Security is all about. After a lifetime of hard work and contribution to this country, do we tell our seniors that they're on their own? Or do we tell them that we're here to help make sure that they have a basic, decent standard of living?

Is the dignity of life in their latter years their problem or one we all share?

Since this is Washington, you won't hear some of these questions answered directly. Instead, what you'll hear is talk of reform. Although what's actually meant is privatization.

You'll hear talk of strengthening which is actually a euphemism for dismantling.

The Cost of Privatization Is High

They will tell us that there's a crisis to get us all riled up, to sit down and listen to their plan to privatize but there's not going to be much discussion about some alternatives that would actually shore up the system.

Here's what we know: Under the president's [George W. Bush's] proposal to privatize, we are looking at cutting guaranteed benefits by at least 40 and up to 50 percent.

We know that the transition costs involved in shifting to a new system would involve borrowing between $2 trillion and $5 trillion from countries like China and Japan.

We know, of course, that fiscal conservatives hate debt and deficit, so we haven't had too much discussion about the specifics of how that would be paid for.

And it's not even about the ability of private accounts to finance the gap on the system. We know that. Even the proponents of privatization have stated that this will not solve the very real funding gap that we'll be experiencing in 35 or 40 years.

So what is this whole thing about? And why have some in power been pushing so hard for so long now? It's probably summed up in one sentence in one White House memo that somehow made its way out of the White House. And I give credit to the White House, this doesn't happen very often.

The Political Agenda

The memo reads: "For the first time in six decades the Social Security battle is one we can win. And in doing so, we can help transform the political and philosophical landscape of the country."

There it is. Since Social Security was first signed into law, almost 70 years ago, . . . at a time when FDR's opponents were calling it a hoax that would never work and that some likened to Communism, there has been movement, there has been movement after movement to get rid of the program for purely ideological reasons.

Because some still believe that we can't solve the problems we face as one American community, they think this country works better when we're left to face fate by ourselves.

Under the . . . proposal to privatize, we are looking at cutting guaranteed benefits by at least 40 and up to 50 percent.

And I understand this view. I understand this perspective. There is something bracing about the social Darwinist idea: the idea that there isn't a problem that the unfettered free market cannot solve. It requires no sacrifice on the part of those of us who've won life's lottery.

It doesn't require us to consider how lucky we are to have the parents we did or the education that we received or the right breaks at the right time.

But I fundamentally disagree with the central premise of what this president has termed the ownership society. And that's what I significantly object to when it comes to the current privatization of Social Security.

What is it exactly that we're going to be telling retirees whose investments in the stock markets have gone badly: that we're sorry; keep working; you're on your own?

When people's expected benefits get cut and they have to choose between groceries and their prescriptions, what will we say then; that's not our problem?

When our debt climbs so high that our children face sky-high taxes, just as they are starting their first job, what are we going to tell them; deal with it?

Real American Values

This isn't how America works. This isn't how we saved millions of seniors from a life of poverty 70 years ago. This isn't how we sent the greatest generation of veterans to college so they could build the greatest middle class in American history. And this isn't how we should face the challenges of the future either.

And yet this is the direction that we are trying to take America in, that those in power are trying to take America in every aspect of public policy.

Instead of trying to contain skyrocketing costs of health care and expand access to the uninsured, we have the health savings account, which basically means that we're going to leave the system alone, eliminate employer-based health care, give you $5,000, and you deal with 15 percent inflation every year.

And I don't know how you deal with it. Well, maybe you just go to the doctor less. That's the idea behind the consumer-driven health care reform model: You go to the doctor less, or you have your child go to the doctor less.

These safety nets are exactly what encourages each of us to be risk-takers.

Instead of strengthening a pension system that provides defined benefits to employees who have worked a lifetime we'll give you a modest tax break. Of course, we'll give you a larger tax break the more money you make and hope that you invest well and save well in your own little account.

And if none of this works, if you can't find affordable insurance or you suffer an illness that leaves you thousands of dollars in debt, then you should no longer count on being able to start over, because we've changed the bankruptcy laws to make sure that the burden of the debt is squarely on your shoulders.

Taking responsibility for one's self, showing individual initiative: These are American values that we all share. Frankly, they are values that we could stand to see more of in a culture where the buck is all too often passed to the next guy. Those are values, by the way, that we could see more of and use more of here in Washington.

Safety Nets Encourage Growth

But the irony of this all-out assault against every existing form of social insurance is that these safety nets are exactly what encourages each of us to be risk-takers, what encourages entrepreneurship, what allows us to pursue our individual ambitions. It happens at the smallest scale and at the largest scale.

We get into our cars knowing that if someone rear ends us, we'll have insurance to pay for the repairs. We buy a house knowing that our investment is protected by homeowner's insurance. We take a chance on start-ups and small businesses, because we know if they fail, there are protections available to cushion our fall.

Corporations obtain limited liability, precisely because we understand that the free market works when people know that utter destitution is not going to be their destination in case their venture fails.

And it's that same reason why we need social insurance to provide people some confidence that in fact as they move around freely pursuing their dreams, pursuing their ambitions, pursuing a vision of what might be accomplished, that they know that they're not in it alone each and every time.

That's how America works. And if we want to keep it working, we need to develop new ways for all of us to share the new risks of a 21st century economy, not destroy those that we already have.

The genius of Roosevelt was putting into practice the idea that America doesn't have to be a place where individual aspirations are at war with our common good; it's a place where one makes the other possible.

Now, I think we will save Social Security from privatization this year. And in doing so, I think we will affirm our belief that we are all connected as one people, ready to share life's risks and rewards for the benefit of each and the good of all.

We need to develop new ways for all of us to share the new risks of a 21st century economy, not destroy those that we already have.

Let me close by suggesting that the Democrats are absolutely united in the need to strengthen Social Security and make it solvent for future generations. We know that, and we want that. And I believe that both Democrats and Republicans can work together to accomplish that.

And while we're at it, we can begin a debate about the real challenges America faces as baby boomers begin to retire: about getting a handle on ever-spiraling health care costs; about increasing individual and national savings; about strengthening our pension system for the 21st century.

These are all important questions that require us to work together, not in a manufactured panic, but in a genuine spirit of solving problems with pragmatism and innovation that will offer every American the secure retirement that they have earned.

You know, there are times in the life of this nation where we are individual citizens, going about our business, enjoying the freedoms that we've been blessed with.

And then there are times when we're one America, linked by the dignity of each and the destiny of all.

Debate over the future of Social Security needs to be one of those latter times.

CHAPTER 4

What Challenges Do the Elderly Face?

Chapter Preface

"Old Geezer" greeting cards and funeral-black party favors announce that someone is "Over the Hill" at the tender age of fifty. These are but a few of the negative messages about aging reflected in American culture. Although birthday cards with such messages are most likely just well-intentioned attempts to poke lighthearted fun at the recipient, some experts claim that these messages are actually thinly veiled expressions of ageism, a type of discrimination based on age, and one of several challenges that the elderly face.

According to International Longevity Center president Robert Butler, who first coined the term in 1968, "The underlying basis of ageism is the dread and fear of growing older, becoming ill and dependent, and approaching death." In her recent book, *Aged by Culture*, ageism critic Margaret Morganroth Gullette adds that from childhood Americans are bombarded with an insidious and false "narrative of decline" that instills negative perceptions about aging. These perceptions are carried and reinforced throughout life. Cultural attitudes about getting old not only play a major role in how elderly people are treated in society but also shape how seniors view themselves.

Some authorities argue that ageism is a pervasive and ubiquitous part of American culture and shapes how the elderly are treated. According to Butler, "ageism is manifested in a wide range of phenomena, on both individual and institutional levels—stereotypes and myths, outright disdain and dislike, simple subtle avoidance of contact, discriminatory practices in housing, employment, and services of all kinds, and of course elder abuse." In the health care system, commentators claim for example, ageist assumptions distort the quality of care for older adults, who as a result often receive less aggressive medical treatments than younger patients. The elderly are also excluded from clinical drug trials, receive fewer screening tests, and are given less access to preventative care. Only one in ten U.S. medical schools require coursework in geriatrics.

In the workplace, studies show that pension cutbacks, golden-handshake layoffs of older workers, and discrimination in hiring are all too common. Older workers are less likely to receive job offers than younger workers with similar qualifications, and they typically receive half as much training as their younger counterparts. Some employers think older workers lack computer skills, and others fear high health insurance costs. "In our youth-oriented society, most human resource practices are often explicitly or implicitly biased against older workers," gerontologist Ken Dychtwald told the Senate Committee on Aging in September 2004. Dychtwald challenges the business world to cast aside its ageist ways and to embrace aging boomers as they redefine the employment landscape in positive ways.

Commentators also claim that the attitudes the elderly have about getting old affect their mental and physical health and longevity. Evidence reveals that elderly people attempt suicide more frequently than any other group and are more likely to succeed in their attempts. Studies also show, however, that those with positive attitudes about aging live 7.5 years longer on average than those with negative attitudes. "Our society," argues Butler, "needs to change the erroneous and hurtful images such as 'geezer' to truer images of older people who are active, flexible, relevant, culturally involved, and an increasingly important segment of our society."

The challenge of ageism, whether obvious or obscured, is a thread that runs through the viewpoints in the following chapter: What Challenges Do the Elderly Face?

Elderly Workers Face Discrimination

Joanna N. Lahey

Joanna N. Lahey is a postdoctoral research fellow with the National Bureau of Economic Research, a private, nonprofit, nonpartisan research organization dedicated to promoting a greater understanding of how the economy works.

As the leading edge of the baby boom generation approaches 60, growing evidence suggests that many may want to work beyond traditional retirement ages. Longer work lives may be desirable for a combination of reasons, including financial need, robust health, and the desire to stay active, productive, and engaged.

Working at Later Ages

Financial need may be the single most important incentive to work longer. Even at today's level of Social Security benefits, many older Americans need to work as they have little income from other sources. Indeed, one-third of those over 65 rely on Social Security for virtually all of their income. A disproportionate share of these Social Security dependent beneficiaries are women. In addition, as baby boomers begin to retire, the need for income will become even more important for two reasons. First, Social Security benefits are expected to replace a smaller share of individuals' pre-retirement income due to increases under current law in the full benefits retirement age, and the need to solve the program's long-term financial shortfall. Second, 401(k) plans have replaced traditional defined benefit plans as the dominant pension vehicle, and accumulations in 401(k)s are likely to be much lower than people expect at retirement.

Fortunately, older Americans are now more capable of working at later ages than in years past. Several studies suggest that today's 70 year olds are comparable in health and mental function to 65 year olds from 30 years ago. In addition to the monetary rewards, work also offers health and psychological benefits. Working in later ages may contribute to an older person's mental acuity and provide a sense of usefulness. Indeed, when surveyed, many people say they wish to continue working at least part time into later ages as a bridge to retirement.

Americans will need to work longer, they are capable of working longer, and many say they wish to work longer. But will they be able to find work at later ages? This brief describes existing evidence on age discrimination and summarizes the results of a recent experiment that found that older job applicants are treated differently than younger applicants. It then explores possible reasons for this differential treatment.

Existing Evidence on Age Discrimination

What, exactly, is discrimination? In its most pure sense, discrimination is simply treating people in one group differently than people in another group, based solely on perceived group characteristics rather than individual differences. The most worrisome type of discrimination is what economists term animus or "taste-based" discrimination. Taste-based discrimination occurs when one group dislikes another group for no good reason. This type of discrimination does not benefit anyone economically. However, another type of discrimination is almost as troubling. This type arises in situations where an employer faces significant costs to find out specific characteristics of an individual applicant or worker. To avoid these costs, the employer may make assumptions about the applicant based on group characteristics. Thus, an employer may assume that a college graduate will be a higher skilled worker than a high school graduate, regardless of actual ability. When this type of discrimination is based on a group-status that a high ability worker can change, such as education level, economists generally do not worry about it. However, when the group in question is based on race, gender, or age, then many high ability workers may be unjustly discriminated against because it is costly for employers to test true ability.

To a casual news reader, it may seem obvious that age discrimination exists. Newspapers are full of stories about people over the age of 50 having difficulty finding jobs or being laid off. Recent class-action suits, such as the one sparked by mass layoffs at Home Depot, make headlines. However, these could merely be isolated cases getting a lot of press attention, specifically because they are so rare.

Additionally, just because older workers are having more trouble finding jobs than younger workers does not mean that firms are systematically choosing not to hire an older worker over a younger worker. Older workers may be used to getting higher wages based on their expertise in a former firm, or what economists term "firm-specific human capital." Once they leave their old firm, they cannot always use the skills that made them an asset to the old firm because the new firm may not need all of those skills. Thus, they may be less valuable to the new firm, and an older worker expecting to be paid the same wage will be unable to find work at that price. Older workers may also be clustered in industries and occupations where demand for workers is lower, or they may have less education on average than younger workers. Any of these situations would lead to older workers having more difficulty finding jobs.

Looking at the Evidence

Until recently, there has been very little evidence to show whether or not age discrimination exists in hiring. One study finds that although most older workers plan to continue working at least part time instead of fully retiring, those who have to change jobs in order to reduce hours are likely to stop working entirely. This finding suggests that workers who would have to switch jobs to cut hours are either more likely to change their minds about working part time or else something prevents them from finding a new job. Another study, which used the Displaced Workers Survey from the Current Population Survey, finds that older workers who have lost their jobs because of lay-offs or plant closings take longer to find a new job than younger workers who have similarly lost their jobs. These findings could be evidence of discrimination against older job seekers. However, it may be that older job seekers are more picky about their wages or the type of employment they are willing to accept than younger seekers.

Psychologists have tested for age discrimination more directly. In studies where undergraduates or human resource managers are given resumes that are identical except for age and asked to hypothetically choose between them, they will usually choose the younger of the two candidates. While these studies are highly suggestive that age discrimination does exist in labor markets, they are not conclusive since they do not measure what is actually going on in the hiring process. For example, since it is illegal to discriminate based on age, even if hiring managers hypothetically prefer younger workers, they may hire the older worker at least some of the time in practice because they fear potential lawsuits.

An Experiment to Test for Age Discrimination

Perhaps the best way to test for age discrimination in the labor market is to enter the labor market itself and look at the genuine reactions of employers faced with choices. In a recent study, I adopted this approach by sending out resumes for job applicants with different ages and measuring the response rate of employers asking for interviews. This type of study is called an Audit study and has been useful in the past for determining race and gender discrimination in labor and housing markets.

The Audit technology does have some limitations. Since it is difficult to find an older person who is identical to a younger person except for age, one cannot actually send people to interview for jobs. Thus, information is only available for the first part of the hiring screening process—from resume to interview. However, studies on gender and race find additional discrimination once the candidates have reached the interview stage, so it is possible that older applicants being interviewed will not be preferred over younger applicants.

A younger worker ... is more than 40 percent more likely to be called back for an interview than an older worker.

The experiment in this particular study involved sending 4000 resumes to firms in Boston, Massachusetts and St. Petersburg, Florida. These resumes were for job applicants between the ages of 35 and 62. Since most people do not actually put their ages on resumes, age was indicated by date of high school graduation. Job listings were found via the local Sunday want-ads and through cold-calling firms listed in local phone books.

Because employers might infer things that could not be measured about the resumes differently for older workers than for younger workers, the study looked at limited types of resumes. To avoid the issue of what employers value in a work history, the experiment only applied to entry-level jobs, or jobs that required up to a year of education and experience combined. These included positions such as clerical work, licensed practical nurse (LPN), air conditioner repair-person, and nail tech. Applicants also have short work histories in more basic entry-level fields such as data entry or fast food. The sample was also limited to women. When an adult man applies for an entry-level job with only a short work history, the employer is likely to think that there is something wrong with him. In the worst case scenario, the employer might think the man had been incarcerated, and the older man incarcerated for longer than the younger with the same resume. With a female applicant, however, employers might plausibly assume that—regardless of age—she has been at home taking care of her family. Since the majority of the jobs applied for are in female-dominated industries, the experiment gives an accurate picture of the job opportunities for one of the most at-risk populations of older workers—recent widows and divorcees.

New Evidence on Age Discrimination

[There is a] downward trend by age of the probability of being called in for an interview in the two cities. A younger worker in either state is more than 40 percent more likely to be called back for an interview than an older worker, where older is defined as age 50 or older. In Massachusetts, this trend translates into a younger seeker needing to send in 19 resumes for one interview request compared to 27 for an older worker. Similarly, in Florida the comparable numbers of resumes are 16 and 23 respectively.

A younger worker will take 6–10 weeks to receive a clerical job offer ... and an older worker will not receive a job offer for 14–20 weeks!

Of course, these numbers are only averages. They include people applying for different types of jobs, as well as resumes that have different educational requirements, such as nursing certificates for those applying for LPN positions or a cosmetology license for hair stylist applicants. Thus, different parts of the population may end up having to send a different number of applications before finding employment. For example, a younger worker qualified as an LPN in Florida would have to respond to 5.5 ads before receiving an interview offer, whereas an older worker would have to respond to 10. In contrast, finding clerical work is harder—in Massachusetts, it takes 32 applications for a younger worker and 72 for an older worker.

Some may argue that applying for a few more jobs imposes no major hardship on an older worker. However, this reasoning assumes that an infinite number of jobs are available. Obviously, they are not. For example, a newspaper for a metropolitan area such as St. Petersburg-Tampa Bay may have two or three dozen ads each week for LPNs or dental assistants, but fewer than 10 ads for pre-school teachers or hair dressers; and some positions—such as gem appraiser—are rarely advertised at all. Additionally, many ads run for more than one week at a time, so a number of ads in any given week are simply repeats from the previous week. So, it may take an older job seeker a considerable time to find a position.

How much longer will it take an older worker to find a job compared to a younger worker, assuming she applies to all applicable ads in the paper every week? If we assume that it takes 7-10 interviews to obtain a position (which may be optimistic, since that is the estimate for college graduates), then a younger LPN will receive a job offer in a week, and an older LPN will only have to wait 3 weeks for a job offer. At the other extreme, a younger worker will take 6-10 weeks to receive a clerical job offer (assuming that half of the ads each week are repeats), and an older worker will not receive a job offer for 14-20 weeks! This wait could be even longer, since a five-month period involves a number of repeat ads; places that advertised and rejected the older worker in month one will advertise again in month five. Thus, employers clearly do treat older workers differently and the impact can be really harmful, especially for those with low savings who most need work.

Why Would Employers Discriminate?

The question of why employers prefer younger workers to older workers is still an open one. It is important to know the answer to this question in order to make appropriate policy recommendations concerning the needs and desires of older job seekers. For example, if the problem is simply an irrational dislike of older people, educating employers or more strictly enforcing discrimination laws in hiring may be appropriate. However, if older workers in general lack certain skills, then additional training programs for these workers may help. If older workers cost the company more in terms of health insurance, a response by government might be warranted—but this issue is complicated.

Table 1 shows a list of the top 10 reasons offered by employers as to why other employers might be reluctant to hire older workers. Some of these reasons do not apply to the entry-level experiment described above. For example, since the length of the career path for entry-level jobs is short, career potential (the most listed reason) should not matter. Salary expectations (reason 5) may also be less of an issue, since these jobs often have set salary schedules. Additionally, the resumes used in the experiment list current work experience, so the new employer should not be worried about the reason why the applicant left the previous job (reason 9).

Some of the other reasons listed can be explored using the experimental framework described above. For example, if employers think that older workers are more likely to lack computer skills than younger workers (a version of reason 7, knowledge and skills obsolescence), an older worker who indicates that she has these skills should face less discrimination.

Table I. Age Discrimination May Occur for Many Reasons

Reasons for Differential Hiring Suggested by
Survey Respondents

1. Shorter career potential (specific human capital investment)
2. Lack energy
3. Costs of health and life insurance and pensions
4. Less flexible/adaptable
5. Higher salary expectations
6. Health risks [may lead to] absences
7. Knowledge and skills obsolescence
8. Block career paths of younger workers
9. Suspicion about competence (why leave job?)
10. Fear of discrimination suit

Rhine, 1984.

In addition, information about computer skills should help the older seeker more than the younger one, because the employer already assumes that the younger seeker has these skills. Similarly, an attendance award on a previous job should alleviate worries that an older worker will have more absences than a similarly qualified younger worker (reason 6). Using this technique of adding information about certain skills or qualities to selected resumes, the study finds that employers may fear a lack of computer skills, but only in the Massachusetts sample. It also finds no evidence that employers are worried about absences.

The experiment tried to test for a few of the other reasons on the list as well, with less success. To see if reason 2, lack of energy, is a reason employers prefer not to hire older workers, some resumes included that the applicant plays a sport. This item turned out to harm both older and younger workers, so it is probably not signaling energy, but rather the likelihood of getting an injury while playing sports over the weekend. Similarly, putting down "I am flexible" or "I am willing to embrace change," as the AARP [American Association of Retired Persons] suggests, to signal flexibility and adaptability (reason 4), actually hurts older workers. Instead of showing flexibility and adaptability, such statements may just be showing that the applicant is a member of the AARP. The remaining reasons for differential treatment could not be tested under this scenario. However, some evidence is available from other studies.

Employers clearly do treat older workers differently and the impact can be really harmful.

A Fear of Lawsuits

Fear of lawsuits under age discrimination laws is one part of the story. Employers may be afraid to hire older workers because older workers can sue under the age discrimination act if they are later fired or fail to be promoted. It is much easier for an employer to avoid these kinds of lawsuits by simply failing to hire an older worker, since the older worker generally cannot prove that he or she has been discriminated against during the hiring stage. Another study I conducted compares labor market outcomes of older people in states where it is easier to sue under age discrimination laws (those with local laws) to older people in states where it is not as easy (those without such laws). State age discrimination laws are important because they allow people more time to file complaints than the federal Equal Employment Opportunity Commission

(EEOC)—300 days versus 180 days—and a state's Fair Employment Practices office can often process claims more quickly than the EEOC.

White older men in states where it is easier to sue are less likely to be hired than such men in states where it is more difficult. They are also less likely to be fired and more likely to say they are retired. Overall, in states where it is easier to sue, older white men work fewer weeks per year than those in states where it is harder to sue. These findings suggest a story in which firms that are in states where it is easier to sue do not wish to hire older men, are afraid to fire older men, and remove older men through strong incentives to retire.

However, fear of lawsuits under age discrimination laws cannot tell the entire story. Ease of lawsuit has no effect on the hiring possibilities for women. This fact could be because older women are the least litigious group in the United States—in general, older women just do not sue. Thus employers do not see potential lawsuits as a possible cost to hiring an older woman.

Other Pieces of the Puzzle

Health insurance and pension costs may be another piece of the puzzle that has not yet been fully explored. One study has found that firms which offer health insurance are less likely to hire older workers than firms that do not. However, this test is imperfect because firms that offer health insurance are very different from those that do not. Not only do firms offering benefits tend to be clustered in different industries, they tend to be larger, have steeper salary schedules and possibly higher levels of productivity. Any of these differences could be a reason for not hiring older workers, regardless of health insurance status. Thus, more work needs to be done in this area.

A final possible reason for differential treatment of older workers, one not mentioned in the survey summarized in Table 1, is an irrational dislike of older people in the workplace. This reason for differential treatment is the first that usually comes to mind when we think of the word "discrimination." It could be that employers just don't want to hire older workers. Or it could be that employees don't like working with older workers. Or people could dislike buying products that older workers are selling. The experiment described earlier tested this possibility by making an assumption that younger people dislike associating with older people more than older people do. This assumption is implicit in the research literature on discrimination but, though plausible, has not been proven to be true. Using this assumption, the study matched the age distribution of an area with the interview rates in the sample by zipcode. This test found that neither the age distribution of employees or of customers in a zipcode has any effect on the interview rates in an area. Thus, the result provided no evidence for this kind of irrational discrimination. However, this method has two problems: first, age distribution information was available only by zipcode rather than by firm, thus preventing an exact match-up with the age composition of the firms doing the hiring. This limitation means that the results are biased toward finding no result, since it is not clear that the test is measuring what it is intended to measure. Second, as noted, the assumption about age preferences may not be true: older and younger people may have no difference in preferences for whom they associate with, or older people may prefer being with younger people to a much greater extent than younger people do.

The evidence . . . paints a picture of age discrimination against older workers in labor markets.

The evidence presented paints a picture of age discrimination against older workers in labor markets. The demand for labor from older workers is smaller than that from younger workers. Simply encouraging older workers to reenter the labor force will not guarantee that they will be able to find jobs in a timely manner, if at all. This finding has important implications for older seekers who are most likely to need work—those who have lost jobs and those with little work experience who unexpectedly need to enter the labor market, such as widows, divorcees, or those whose spouses have lost jobs.

More research needs to be done to ferret out exactly why employers prefer younger workers. Any plan which requires older people to find employment in order to maintain a quality of life needs to consider the demand for older workers and the reasons employers may discriminate against this group.

The Elderly Are Vulnerable to Abuse

National Council on Child Abuse and Family Violence

The National Council on Child Abuse and Family Violence is a nonprofit organization dedicated to understanding and preventing intergenerational violence.

Elder abuse is an often unnoticed yet growing problem in the American culture.

The number of older persons in American society is increasing, with the number of persons over the age of 85 growing faster than the elderly population in general.

With the advancements in medical science contributing to the elongation of the life span for larger numbers of men and women, the challenge of insuring safe, healthy, productive lives for the elderly grows.

For many older persons, the prospect of an extended life means additional suffering and hardship due to abuse or neglect. Victims often live in isolation where their limited physical capacity, fear and increased vulnerability compound their sense of aloneness leading to a decline in their physical, emotional and mental health. Many of these victims suffer in silence, fearful of what will happen to them should the abuse become known.

Prior to the early 1980's the literature on family violence contained limited references to the abuse of elders by their adult children, other family members or caretakers. In the intervening years numerous researchers and scores of professionals have been exploring this dimension of family violence.

The National Statistics Are Alarming

A look at national statistics confirms that many among the aged in our society are victims of elder abuse:

In 1990 the results of two incidence studies were released which involved surveys of state adult protective services and aging agencies nationwide.

The findings indicate that between 1.6 and 2 million older Americans become victims of abuse or neglect in domestic and institutional settings each year.

The U.S. House of Representatives Select Committee on Aging has reported that women are the most likely victims of elder abuse as well as persons 75 years and older, and individuals who are dependent on others for care and protection.

In the past the prospect of caring for an aging adult or elderly parent over a prolonged period of time was not given much consideration by most American families.

Between 1.6 and 2 million older Americans become victims of abuse or neglect in domestic and institutional settings each year.

Today, situations where older persons become the victims of abuse by family members are increasing as greater numbers of parents live into old age and require care from their children.

In a family where there is a tendency to physically harm members who are weak or dependent, the aging members of society, who are among the most vulnerable, become the next victims in the cycle of intergenerational family violence.

Violence toward the elderly by their middle-aged children or others is a special form of family violence and, just like child abuse and domestic violence, deserves to be recognized, investigated and appropriate interventions provided to save victims from unnecessary suffering. Above all, we must educate the public to recognize elder abuse as a devastating form of family violence and work to prevent its occurrence.

What Is Elder Abuse?

The term "elder abuse" is used to describe the mistreatment of older persons in both home and institutional settings. Although a precise and uniform definition of elder abuse does not currently exist, it is generally defined as any unnecessary suffering, whether self-inflicted or other-inflicted, which negatively affects the quality of life of the older person.

Elder abuse is linked to child abuse and domestic/spousal abuse in the chain of intrafamilial violence known as intergenerational family violence. The first documentation of elder abuse in the United States occurred in 1978. Since then increased attention has been given to this growing social problem.

Research and studies into this area of family violence have identified types of abuse and a range of behaviors included in the general concept of elder abuse. We now know that elder abuse victims frequently evidence symptoms similar to victims of the battered child or battered wife syndrome.

It is important to remember that violence and its related behaviors are learned and often passed from one generation to the next. A child who is abused by a parent may become an adult who uses violence toward a spouse or child then, as caretaker for an aging parent, extends the abuse to his/her parent or relative.

What Constitutes Elder Abuse?

The four most common forms of elder abuse are physical abuse (including sexual abuse), psychological and emotional abuse, financial/material abuse, and neglect.

Physical Abuse: Includes behavior toward an elderly person which results in bodily harm, injury, unnecessary pain, unreasonable confinement, punishment, coercion, or mental distress.

Examples of physical abuse include: the infliction of injury, such as dislocation or bone fracture; slapping, cuts, burns; bruises, especially if several exist of different colors which may indicate repeated injuries; bites, lacerations, pushing, shoving, kicking; dehydration or loss of weight without a medical explanation; untreated bedsores or poor skin hygiene, etc.

Also included are the use of physical restraints for punishment, in the case of victims in long-term care facilities, and unnecessary pulling, tugging or twisting of the body by the staff when working with the older resident. Sometimes signs of physical abuse are not obvious and may be camouflaged by clothing or blankets.

Sexual Abuse: Includes any form of sexual contact that results from threats, force or the inability of the older person to give consent, including assault, rape and sexual harassment.

Psychological/Emotional Abuse: This form of abuse includes threats or actions directed at an elderly person in an effort to provoke the fear of violence or isolation and which may result in mental anguish, anxiety or depression.

Examples of psychological abuse include the intentional use of threat or injury, unreasonable confinement, punishment, verbal intimidation or humiliation, name-calling, insulting, frightening, threatening or isolating, yelling or screaming at the older person, using ridicule or demeaning language toward him/her, etc.

Although psychological abuse is more difficult to detect, resultant behaviors may be observable. These behaviors on the part of the victim include withdrawal, depression, anxiety, hesitancy to talk openly about what is going on, denial of the abuse, social isolation from friends or neighbors, and fear of family members.

Financial/Material Abuse: Included in this form of abuse is any behavior by a relative or caregiver, without the knowledge and consent of the older person, that results in financial exploitation of the older person through illegal or unethical use of his/her money, property or other assets for personal gain. Lack of necessities such as food, clothing, a wheelchair, hearing aid, etc., or care that is not consistent with resources available may be symptoms of financial abuse.

Other examples of financial/material abuse include theft or conversion of money, personal or other property to the benefit, gain or profit of the perpetrator and loss to the older adult, such as unusual bank account activity or changes in the title to property.

Neglect: Neglect can be either active or passive on the part of the caregiver. Active neglect means the willful deprivation of goods or services which are necessary to maintain the physical or mental health of the older person. Passive neglect is failing to recognize the elder's needs, thereby keeping from them needed goods and services.

Additional examples of neglect include: a breach of duty or carelessness that results in injury or violation of the older persons' rights, deliberate abandonment; denial of food, medication, or health related services. Serious neglect can occur without a conscious attempt to inflict physical or emotional stress.

What Causes Elder Abuse?

Widely held negative attitudes and dehumanizing stereotypes make older persons vulnerable to maltreatment by both family members and institutional care providers.

Since violence is a learned behavior, if an adult was abused by his/her parents s/he may abuse their aging parents.

Most elder abuse victims are dependent on the abuser for basic needs. The victim may be suffering from a physical or mental impairment, common among the very old, and exhibit behavior indicating fear, withdrawal, depression or helplessness. This situation often leads to dependence upon family members or caregivers who may not be emotionally, financially, or otherwise able to meet these demands.

Resentments, exhaustion and/or guilt can be contributors to the use of abusive behavior.

How Can Elder Abuse Be Prevented?

The prevention of elder abuse is dependent on numerous factors. Among the most important is national re-education and change in attitude toward the elderly and disabled in our society. In addition, we must develop a greater awareness among the public about the nature and scope of elder abuse.

We must educate the public to recognize elder abuse as a devastating form of family violence and prevent its occurrence.

Over the last several years national policy toward the aging has encompassed measures toward the prevention of elder abuse. However, additional work must be done in the development of programs to help families who must or wish to care for elderly members at home. The development of more resources to provide meals, day care, transportation, counseling and help with daily tasks are needed to lessen the stress on both the caregivers and the elderly in need.

With continued research into the causes and treatment of elder abuse, and ongoing prevention education efforts, elder abuse will no longer remain a hidden disgrace.

The Elderly Have High Suicide Rates

Lauren Neergaard

Lauren Neergaard writes for the Associated Press, a newspaper wire service.

Dr. Allan Anderson remembers with frustration how the retired professional who was losing his eyesight calmly explained he would kill himself once he became blind.

He didn't wait that long.

Senior citizens commit suicide at higher rates than any other age group, and with graying Baby Boomers—already more prone to suicide than other generations—entering the riskiest years, psychiatrists fear that could soon worsen.

Now researchers are uncovering factors—such as lack of social support, poor sleep patterns, and memory or other brain problems that sometimes hit seniors—that could help primary care physicians spot elderly patients at risk of suicide and intervene.

It's hard: Many of today's seniors are the generation of the stiff upper lip when it comes to mental health. Ask how they're feeling and you may hear a litany about aching joints, but they're far less likely than younger people to admit to depression, said Anderson, a geriatric psychiatrist in Cambridge, Md.

That leaves doctors and loved ones to notice subtle clues like a senior not discussing a much-beloved hobby anymore—or to struggle to help the elderly surmount a daunting physical loss, like Anderson's patient who had no family to lean on when his vision faded.

Suicides Are Preventable

Most are not terminally ill, and thus these are largely preventable deaths, insists Dr. Yeates Conwell, a University of Rochester specialist in elderly suicide.

"We tend to seek the simple solution: Mr. Smith killed himself because his wife died or Mrs. Jones killed herself because she was diagnosed with cancer," but that's seldom the real reason, he said. "We have to go beyond simple explanations and start looking . . . at the tapestry of older people's lives."

Americans 65 and older account for about 13 percent of the population but almost a fifth of all suicides. The national rate is 11 suicides for every 100,000 people, about the same for teens. But the risk steadily rises with age—and most at risk are older white men: 33 of every 100,000 of them commit suicide every year, translating to 4,655 suicides in 1998 alone.

Senior citizens commit suicide at higher rates than any other age group.

Contrast that with older black women: In 1998, fewer than 20 killed themselves, yielding a suicide rate too small to reliably compute, University of Pennsylvania researchers report in [the July 2002] *American Journal of Geriatric Psychiatry*.

What explains those dramatic differences—and could psychiatrists harness whatever protected the black women into some sort of therapy for other seniors at risk?

Scientists don't yet know for sure. But new research reported in the geriatric psychiatry journal shows while depression is a clear risk at any age, there are some special senior warning signs. No specific illness was associated with suicide, but perceived poor health is—as is poor sleep quality and having fewer friends or relatives to confide in.

Memory or other brain problems may play a role, too.

In contrast, strong ties to social and religious support networks may be the key protection for older black women.

Whatever the cause, senior suicide attempts are strikingly lethal. Four elders attempt suicide for each who succeeds. That compares with 200 attempts per completed suicide among young adults, who may have planned the attempt less carefully or may have more family or friends around to find and revive them.

Worsening the problem is the myth that it's normal to feel sad or depressed when you get old. Too often, Conwell laments, even doctors believe that myth and don't diagnose treatable depressive illnesses.

"Your doctor can only treat you if you say how you're really feeling," advises the National Institute of Mental Health, which urges seniors to seek help for symptoms including:

- Feeling nervous, "empty," worthless, tired, restless or irritable.

- Not enjoying things like they used to, or feeling no one loves them or that life isn't worth living.

- Eating or sleeping more or less than normal.

- Having persistent headaches, stomach aches or chronic pain.

Most seniors who commit suicide had seen a primary care physician in the previous month, and psychiatrists urge those doctors to look for clues. Ask "What thoughts have you had about suicide?" instead of the easier-to-evade "Are you depressed?" advises Anderson—and consult a mental health specialist immediately about any patient deemed at risk.

The Elderly Are Vulnerable to Financial Exploitation

Susanna Schrobsdorff

Susanna Schrobsdorff writes for Newsweek, *a national weekly newsmagazine.*

Kerry Sprague didn't have a clue that her mother-in-law, Eleanor Sprague, was giving thousands of dollars to phony charities. Then one day, Eleanor, who was 82, told Kerry that she was upset because a charity was asking her to leave big donations under her doormat. "That was a red flag," explains Kerry. "We checked up on her a lot, but it wasn't until she started complaining that we knew something was wrong."

Eleanor had been living independently in a three-bedroom ranch-style house in Lafayette, Colo., five minutes away from her son and daughter-in-law. A former bookkeeper, she was good with money, but sometime during the summer of 2003, vascular dementia impaired her judgment and she was taken advantage of by scam artists who conned her out of $24,000, according to her daughter-in-law. "They just happened to get her at the right time," says Kerry, who says she verified her fears by checking the phone numbers on the fake receipts from phony charities. "We had mom over to dinner every week, you would think we would have seen the signs of the dementia, but we didn't," she adds.

There are millions of older victims like Eleanor Sprague. The nonprofit National Center on Elder Abuse estimates that there are 5 million cases of elder financial exploitation annually, with most going unreported by seniors either too embarrassed about being duped or unaware the theft is happening. With an asset-rich bubble of baby boomers heading into their golden years, advocates are preparing for what could be the perfect setup for elder fraud on a massive scale. By 2030, the number of elderly is expected to nearly double to 71.5 million people—a whopping 20 percent of the total U.S. population, according to the U.S. Administration on Aging. Many of these aging boomers have money. Currently people over 50 control 70 percent of the nation's wealth. In their later, vulnerable years, they will be obvious targets for corrupt telemarketers, lottery scammers and worse yet, unethical relatives and friends.

"There is going to be a criminal explosion in the next 10 years in this demographic," says Paul Greenwood, a deputy district attorney in San Diego and an expert on elder fraud. The ominous statistics are worrying lawmakers enough that new measures are being proposed to track and prevent financial scams against seniors. At the moment, there is a patchwork of state and federal legislation and very little national data. Even the definition of "elderly" varies from state to state, and many law-enforcement agencies, including the FBI, don't have statistics on financial fraud victims' ages. "We just don't have these numbers," says FBI crime-victim advocate Debbie Deem. "But anyone who is working crimes like telemarketing fraud or investment fraud would tell you that these crimes impact [the elderly]. I can mention only two telemarketing victims that were not elderly in my years of investigating thousands of cases. That's just who they target." According to the FBI, telemarketing fraud across all age groups costs the nation about $40 billion annually.

The Elder Justice Act

The trend has prompted Sens. Orrin Hatch, Republican of Utah, and Blanche Lincoln, Democrat of Arkansas, to sponsor the Elder Justice Act for introduction in the [2006] Congress. The act proposes elevating elder crime (financial, physical and emotional) to the same importance nationally as crimes against women and children. "I don't think Americans talk about elder abuse or are really aware that these egregious acts are occurring every day to our senior citizens," says Senator Hatch. "This bill will raise that awareness, which is almost half the battle right there." Those working for passage of the bill hope that it will result in better tracking of the problem on a federal level, better funding for overburdened adult protective services units in each state, as well as training for law enforcement so that the crimes against the elderly can be better recognized and prosecuted. And, as advocates point out, even if the federal government doesn't come up with funds to prevent elder financial exploitation, we are likely to be paying anyway since seniors who've been bankrupted often become dependent on government programs.

There are 5 million cases of elder financial exploitation annually, with most going unreported by seniors.

Some states faced with large elderly populations are taking action now. [In July 2005], financial institutions, prosecutors and elder advocates in California, which is home to the nation's largest elderly population, reached agreement on a bill that would require employees in financial institutions to report suspicions of exploitation of the elderly and dependent adults. Other professions like clergy and even animal-control officers are already required to report suspicions of elder abuse under threat of criminal penalties. The compromise requires the bank employee to make the report but holds the institution, not the individual employee, subject to civil fines (rather than criminal) for failing to report. Fewer than half of all states have passed laws requiring this kind of reporting by financial institutions.

Proponents hope for a vote on the banking bill in September [2005]. "Sometimes the monthly trip to the bank is the only social contact the elderly have," says Frank Mecca, executive director of the County Welfare Directors Association, which represents human-services directors in California's 58 counties. "Banks can provide early warning that a senior is being victimized. Once they've been fleeced it's almost impossible to get the money back." Mecca's group says that reports of elderly financial abuse in California have increased by 47 percent [from 2000 to 2005].

In their later, vulnerable years, [the elderly] will be obvious targets for corrupt telemarketers, lottery scammers and worse yet, unethical relatives and friends.

New Ways to Prosecute

Besides legislative efforts, California is using the judicial system in new ways to pursue those who defraud elders. In a groundbreaking case, Melissa McKowan, a deputy district attorney in San Mateo County, won a larceny conviction in August 2004 against Ronald Brock who stole approximately $661,000 from a 76-year-old man who was suffering from cognitive impairment. McKowan convinced the court that Brock knew that the elderly man lacked the capacity to resist Brock's request for the money. She charged that Brock used "undue influence," a definition usually used in civil court, to defraud a vulnerable citizen. "In civil court when you have undue influence, you simply rescind the transaction and return everyone to their original positions, but what we're saying is that's not enough," McKowan explains. "We're saying that the impairment was so obvious that it is larceny." Brock's lawyers are in the process of preparing an appeal. If the conviction holds, it may open the door for other cases where law enforcement might want to challenge questionable gifts by an impaired elderly person to an acquaintance, relative or friend. The National Center on Elder Abuse reports that "non-stranger" exploitation makes up a majority of elder fraud cases.

One of the problems for prosecutors is that elderly victims often die or lose the capacity to testify before a case gets to trial. To help elderly witnesses, San Diego Deputy District Attorney Paul Greenwood provides wheelchairs, walkers, oxygen machines, hearing devices and specially equipped vans. "I love putting a 95-year-old witness on," he says. "If they are forgetful, the jury sees their vulnerability." Greenwood says enforcement can't keep up with the cases they're seeing. "I think the crooks are winning. We need the Elder Justice Act desperately." Greenwood is also pressing for mandatory background checks of all caregivers for the elderly.

Fraud Cases Are Not Simple

No one knows how difficult it is to prosecute these crimes better than the family of Eleanor Sprague. With the help of AARP ElderWatch, a Colorado group that coordinates services for elder abuse victims, Kerry Sprague organized a sting operation whereby the alleged charity scammers came to her mother-in-law's house and were arrested by waiting detectives. But charges of theft originally levied against the two men, Rhett Cline and Jay Wyss, in 2003 were dismissed in 2004 pending further investigation by the Boulder County district attorney's office. "This is a very active investigation," says Timothy Johnson, deputy district attorney. "But these are not simple cases like someone goes into a store and steals money out of a register. It takes a tremendous amount of time to put together evidence like bank records."

Kerry says that immediately after the scam, the family had to make the heartbreaking decision to get power of attorney so they could restrict access to Eleanor's bank accounts. "Everything snowballed after that," remembers Kerry. "She was very angry when we had to take her checking account away. The whole thing was humiliating for her, but she spoke to [investigators] so that no one else would have to go through this." Eleanor has since died.

The FBI's Deem expects to see an increase in these cases. "The opportunities for fraud are so much more than 20 years ago. Now [criminals] can get you so many ways. It's not like the old days when they used to go by with their wagons of snake oil. Now they can find you through the mail or through their [phone] databases or through the Internet." Fraudulent telemarketers may spend months cultivating their victims with daily phone calls. Some even send birthday cards. So, when the betrayal comes, it's all the more wrenching. Deem says that many of the elderly victims she deals with get extremely depressed. "This can destroy them emotionally as well as financially," she says. "Some tell me they want to commit suicide. It's such an insidious evil to drain them of everything in their last years. I call it the final indignity."

The Elderly Lack Affordable Housing

James J. Callahan Jr.

James J. Callahan Jr. is a professor and director of the Policy Center for Aging at the Heller School for Social Policy and Management at Brandeis University. He is a former secretary of the Massachusetts Department of Elder Affairs.

Older people want to remain independent and live in their own homes—in other words, age in place. In the past 15 years, aging in place has become a reality for more older people, as state home-care programs, Medicare home-health services, Medicaid personal-care programs, and residential alternatives have expanded. Evidence of this is the fact that in 1999 there were about 200,000 fewer nursing home residents than expected, had the 1985 rate of institutionalization continued.

One of the promising residential alternatives is assisted living. This industry, serving primarily higher-income elders, grew quickly in the 1990s and, in some parts of the country, has reached saturation. Assisted living companies, moreover, have seen declining stock prices as the growth spurt ended. If the industry is to continue to grow, and if lower- and moderate-income people are to have access, "affordable" assisted living must be developed.

Affordability Is the Key

"Affordable" means people earning less than 50 to 60 percent of the area's median income can afford to pay the rent. Service costs—personal assistance, housekeeping, meals—must be covered by Medicaid. The rent is made affordable through subsidies that may include Housing Finance Agency tax-exempt bonds, low income housing tax credits, rental assistance, and federal and state housing programs. Knowledgeable housing finance personnel are necessary to put the financing package together, and skilled providers are needed to design the services. The receipt of housing subsidies and public service programs threatens to undercut the philosophy of assisted living.

Assisted living is based on the concept of aging in place with services provided to maintain one's ability to live at home. The older person should have the same autonomy, capacity to choose, and privacy as if she lived in her own apartment or single-family home. To achieve these goals, assisted living facilities usually have resident contracts, shared risk agreements, and limits on access to a person's apartment. The threat to this philosophy arises from the growing frailty of assisted living residents and the natural tendency of government to regulate the use of its subsidies and program dollars.

Affordable assisted living [for the elderly] will and should continue to grow, . . . but it is not the only model for combining housing and services.

If the frailty levels of residents are too high, the LIHTC [Low Income Housing Tax Credit] and the IRS [Internal Revenue Service] may consider residences to be nursing facilities and thus ineligible for certain subsidies. Medicaid programs may question whether the facility is staffed adequately to meet resident needs. Private insurers, worried about their liability, may raise premiums or walk away from providing coverage. Owners may demand that rent subsidies be paid directly to them rather than the older person—thus reducing autonomy. An unfortunate event in one of these facilities could result in more government regulation. Safety would take priority over personal autonomy.

Assisted Living Is Not the Only Model

Affordable assisted living will and should continue to grow, despite concerns that it may become more institution-like. But it is not the only model for combining housing and services. Many states, particularly Massachusetts, have an extensive housing and services program that brings personal assistance into public housing and private subsidized developments. These programs largely avoid the regulatory rules imposed on free standing assisted living facilities. HUD [U.S. Department of Housing and Urban Development], for example, is supporting reconfiguration of some of its senior housing to permit more intensive services.

States should focus programs on geographic areas, such as census tracts where 50 percent or more of residents are 65 or older. Residents of these "natural occurring retirement communities" age in place, and services could be more efficiently organized utilizing economies of scale.

A public policy that successfully addresses aging in place must include a broad array of residential and service programs, of which affordable assisted living is one, but not the only, option.

Lack of Transportation Options Restrict Elderly Independence

In Hee Choi et al.

In Hee Choi is a doctoral student at the University of Southern California (USC), in Los Angeles. Phoebe Liebig is an associate professor of gerontology and public administration at USC. Dawn Alley is a doctoral candidate in gerontology at USC. Jon Pynoos is United Parcel Service Professor of Gerontology, Policy, Planning and Development at USC.

Mobility is a central issue for older adults who are aging in place. Mobility in the community often depends on the built environment and on transportation services, most of which were not designed to support use by a high number of older adults. Creating communities that support mobility for elders thus requires further planning and infrastructure development.

The term *elder-friendly community* generally refers to a place where elders are actively involved, valued and supported with infrastructures and services that effectively accommodate their changing needs. Studies conducted by the National Resource Center on Supportive Housing and Home Modification have identified accessible and affordable transportation, accessible public buildings, streets designed both for safe walking and for safe driving, and adequate pedestrian and traffic controls as some of the most important characteristics of elder-friendly communities.

In Hee Choi, Phoebe Liebig, Dawn Alley, and Jon Pynoos, "Elder-Friendly Communities Enhance Mobility," *American Society on Aging MAX Newsletter,* vol. 12, Winter 2005, pp. 2, 8. Copyright © 2005 by the American Society on Aging, San Francisco, CA. Reproduced by permission. www.asaging.org.

How Seniors Get Around

The three most important means of mobility in American communities are private automobiles, public transportation and walking. Following is an overview of ways in which community planners can adapt each of these modes into more elder-friendly forms.

Private Automobiles. The private automobile is the most common form of transportation among all age groups in the United States. Indeed, today's elders are more automobile-oriented than ever. An AARP [American Association of Retired Persons] study done in 1999 reported that people over age 65 make more than 90 percent of their trips by private vehicle, either as a driver or a passenger. At the same time, older drivers often report difficulties with seeing street signs, crossing intersections, following road markings and responding to traffic signals.

Furthermore, functional limitations often force older adults to modify their driving behavior, limit trips or rely on rides from family members. Given these circumstances, improved designs for roads and traffic facilities, as well as easy-to-read signage, can provide an appropriate balance of mobility and safety for all road users, but particularly for older adults.

Public Transportation. One alternative to the private automobile for older adults is public transit, which can range from fixed-route bus and rail lines to flexible door-to-door van services to more personal service provided by volunteer drivers. In contrast to the private automobile, however, public transportation connects fewer origins and destinations, generally provides service at more limited times and requires certain levels of physical and cognitive ability for its use.

Providing an appropriate mix of efficient, easy-to-use, innovative transportation services to older adults has been an ongoing challenge for local and state agencies and service providers. The availability of options varies across communities, and the programs vary greatly in terms of funding and design. Furthermore, coordination among the various systems often is lacking, making it difficult to determine what programs exist and to establish who is eligible to use them and under what circumstances.

Martin Wachs, director of the Institute of Transportation Studies at the University of California, Berkeley, suggests the following steps for improving public transit systems:

- Developing collaboration among clients and social service agencies responsible for planning the complex mix of transit and paratransit services offered in communities.

- Increasing coordination among public, private and nonprofit agencies involved in mobility and transportation.

- Funding further research and encouraging experimentation with a wide variety of transportation programs.

Walking. Walking is the second most common mode of transportation for older adults. Yet walkers, too, face challenges: Public and private spaces in communities contain numerous hazards—such as irregular surfaces, obstacles in walkways or poor lighting—and often lack supportive features such as handrails. These environmental hazards and deficits impede older pedestrians' safety and have been identified as potential risk factors for falls among older adults. Communities can make pedestrian environments safe and accessible by eliminating hazardous conditions and by adding supportive features, such as clearly marked crosswalks, signals that allow elders ample time to cross and more benches for resting.

Future Directions and Opportunities

Communities seeking to be elder friendly should offer a variety of transportation options and develop a pedestrian-friendly, barrier-free environment. To accomplish these goals, planners should take into consideration elders' need to select among various modes of transportation based on their particular capacities and situations. In addition, federal, state and local jurisdictions need to work together to support a wide range of innovative, customer-friendly transportation options and to encourage research on improving service quality.

Communities can make pedestrian environments safe and accessible [for the elderly] by eliminating hazardous conditions.

Community settings can be made more friendly to older adults by adopting the concepts of universal accessibility and universal design, which make the built environment safer, more accessible and more adaptable. Such efforts also can benefit from emerging paradigms in contemporary urban planning that emphasize the importance of mixed land use— placing services in close proximity to residences, fostering higher density development and encouraging more pedestrian-oriented designs and activities. The result will be communities that are friendlier for all residents and that enable elders to enjoy increased quality of life while remaining in their own homes and communities as long as possible.

Ageism Remains a Serious Problem for the Elderly

Abigail Trafford

Abigail Trafford writes a weekly column about health and aging issues for the Washington Post.

"**D**id you hear about the miracle drug, Gingko Viagra?"
"No, what does it do?"

"It helps you remember what the #!?*! you're doing."

Ha, ha, ha. But once the laughter dies down, here's the bad news: Jokes like these are hazardous to your health. They increase your risk of heart disease, lower your performance on cognitive tests, accelerate memory loss and impede your will to live. They even make your handwriting worse.

Those are the findings from recent research into the health consequences of chronic exposure to negative stereotypes about aging. From advertisements to greeting cards, subtle and not-so-subtle messages create an image of the elderly as forgetful, slow, sexless, incompetent, debilitated, dependent, childlike, near death. In our youth-obsessed society, anti-aging stereotypes get ingrained by about age 6.

Trouble is, ageism can make you sick. A new study from Yale University shows just how a geezer-bashing culture can damage a person's mental and physical functioning. Researchers divided 54 men and women between the ages of 62 and 82 into two groups. With a technique called subliminal priming, words were flashed across a computer screen. Participants could perceive the flash but not identify the words. In one group, the messages were all negative, with words such as "Alzheimer's," "confused," "decline," "decrepit," "dementia," "forgets," "misplaces" and "senile." In the other group, the words were positive—"accomplished," "alert," "astute," "creative," "enlightened," "guidance," "insightful," "sage," "wise."

Those who got negative messages experienced significant increases in blood pressure that lasted for half an hour—a [response that] concerned researchers because high blood pressure increases the risk of heart attack and stroke. They also showed a greater response to stress, according to skin measurements.

"This suggests that the negative stereotyping people encounter in their daily lives can have an impact on physiological functioning," says Becca R. Levy, an assistant professor of epidemiology and public health at Yale University.

What's more, participants in the negative-message group performed worse on mathematical tests. And they had more difficulty on a verbal test in which they had to recount a stressful experience in the past five years.

Levy speculates that the constant bombardment of negative stereotypes in the culture gets internalized by older people, which lowers their expectations of performance. Doing badly on a test—appearing like a dim-witted old geezer—becomes a self-fulfilling prophecy.

Negative messages are so endemic you scarcely notice them—as long as you're not "old." A grown daughter takes her mother for a medical checkup, and the doctor directs all conversation to the daughter, as though the mother were a child or not even there. A sixty-ish couple is out on the dance floor, cheek to cheek, and someone says: Isn't that cute! As though the couple were two toddlers up past their bedtime.

Greeting cards reinforce the dread of getting older. "Hang in there, Earth creature," says the friendly space alien on one card, "It's only a birthday—not the end of the solar system."

It doesn't have to be this way. The Yale study also shows that positive age stereotypes can protect people from stress.

Certainly other countries have more respect for older people. The Chinese, for example, have a much more positive attitude toward aging. In a 1994 study by Levy and her colleagues, older participants in China performed much better on memory tests than their American counterparts. In fact, the Chinese elderly scored just as high as the young Chinese participants.

This raises the possibility that the much-heralded memory decline associated with age in the absence of disease has more to do with negative stereotyping than with any biological determinism.

Humor has always been an antidote to pain. But making the elderly the butt of jokes is bad medicine.

In a subsequent study of 90 men and women in New England, Levy found that, as expected, the group primed with negative messages did poorly on memory tests. The flip side is that those given positive messages did well. "Memory decline is not inevitable," concludes Levy. "In fact, the studies show that memory performance can be enhanced in old age."

You wouldn't know that from the jokes circulating about older people.

"Hey, I saw they were having these classes in memory improvement down at the senior center."

"I go every week. I'm learning these great tricks."

"Oh, yeah. Like what?"

"You know. What's the name of a flower that has a long stem, many thorns, is brightly colored and very fragrant?"

"A rose."

"That's it!" He turns to his wife and says: "Rose, what were some of those tricks they were teaching us in memory class?"

Very funny. But medically bogus. Forgetting the name of your wife is not a feature of aging, but a sign of disease. Do we really want to make fun of sick people?

Humor has always been an antidote to pain. But making the elderly the butt of jokes is bad medicine.

Not so long ago people used to laugh at racial and gender jokes. But not anymore—not in public anyway. "It's shocking that we are permitting a level of negative humor with the elderly that disappeared at the racial and gender level two decades ago," says geriatrician Jesse Roth, professor of medicine at Johns Hopkins University School of Medicine. "We're allowing words to describe the elderly that would cause you to lose your job if they were associated with gender or race."

The problem is ageism. And that's no joke.

The Elderly Face a Lack of Compassion

George Neumayr

George Neumayr is executive editor of the American Spectator, *a conservative newsmagazine.*

Editor's note: In 1729 Jonathan Swift wrote the oft-cited satirical essay "A Modest Proposal for Preventing the Children of Poor People in Ireland from Being a Burden to Their Parents or Country, and for Making Them Beneficial to the Public." Swift suggested that the Irish eat the nation's poor children so that they would no longer be a burden on the social welfare system. To draw attention to America's lack of compassion toward the elderly, in the following viewpoint George Neumayr offers his own satirical "Modest Proposal" for keeping the disabled and elderly from being a burden to their families and an already strained Medicare system.

It is a melancholy object to those who travel in America when they see the hospices and hospitals crowded with the disabled and elderly. These people, instead of being able to work for their honest livelihood or even show signs of meaningful mental life, impose severe burdens on the healthy.

I think it is agreed by all parties, at least within America's mainstream, that this prodigious number of disabled and elderly in the arms, or on the backs, or at the heels of their family members, and frequently of their isolated and deprived husbands, is in the present deplorable state of the country with its deficits, unsustainable Medicare costs, and Social Security crisis a very great additional grievance; and, therefore, whoever could find out a fair, cheap, and easy method of euthanizing this class of the ill would deserve so well of the public as to have his statue set up for a preserver of the nation.

There is a great advantage in this scheme, that it will prevent those undignified lingering deaths of those with no hope of recovery, and that horrid practice of husbands murdering their wives, alas! too frequent among us!

I have been assured by a very knowing Democrat of my acquaintance in Washington, that a disabled person can be dehydrated to death in eight to 12 days. It is not improbable that some scrupulous person might be apt to censure such a practice (although indeed very unjustly and unconstitutionally), as a little bordering upon cruelty; which, I confess, has always been with me the strongest objection against any project, however so well intended.

[The] prodigious number of disabled and elderly . . . is in the present deplorable state of the country . . . a very great additional grievance.

Yet many Americans of searching conscience, many of them Democrats who have long supported the Special Olympics, are sincerely concerned about that vast number of disabled, who are aged, diseased, or irreversibly maimed. It is very well known in the medical schools and courts of this country that these disabled will not recover and can't pursue lives of discernible purpose as any fair-minded magistrate would determine it, and thus the country and most importantly themselves are happily delivered from the indignity of disability by starvation, dehydration, or injection.

If nothing else, this scheme would greatly lessen the number of papists and back-sliding Protestants in America, with whom we are yearly overrun, who pollute hospitals on purpose with a design to deliver America to a "culture of life." Many other advantages might be enumerated. For instance, the liberation of millions of dollars in Medicare fees with which to finance new Viagra payments for seniors not yet disabled.

I can think of no one objection, that will possibly be raised against this proposal, unless it should be urged, that the number of innocent people will be thereby much lessened in America, a risible objection at a time of obvious overpopulation. Let no man talk of selling our country and consciences for nothing, until he has at least some glimpse of hope that research on crushed embryos will cure the disabled and has a hearty and sincere commitment to put that research into practice.

Before anyone advances a proposal in contradiction to my scheme, I desire the author or authors will be pleased maturely to consider two points. First, as things now stand, how they will be able to find Medicare resources for the millions of useless mouths and backs. And, secondly, recognize that there are thousands and thousands of disabled throughout this country, whose whole subsistence put into a common stock would leave us in debt billions of dollars.

I desire these politicians who dislike my overture, and may perhaps be so bold as to attempt an answer, that they will first ask the spouses of these mortals, whether they would not at this day think it a great happiness to have been starved for the sake of a death with dignity, thereby avoiding such a perpetual scene of misfortunes as they have since gone through by the oppression of their infirmity or age, the impossibility of sharing the costs their families must carry to care for them, and the most inevitable prospect of entailing the like or greater miseries upon their family for ever.

Glossary

activities of daily living (ADLs) Activities necessary for an individual to take care of themselves independently. ADLs include bathing, eating, dressing, grooming, going to the toilet, taking medication, and transferring from a bed to chair. See also, **instrumental activities of daily living (IADLs)**.

ageism Discrimination against a person or a group of people because of their age.

aging in place Growing old in one's own home rather than in a nursing home or other facility for the elderly.

Alzheimer's disease A type of dementia that results in a loss of mental functions due to the deterioration of brain tissue. Those who have it lose their memory and become unable to recognize familiar surroundings or people. It is a progressive disease that ultimately leads to death. About 4.5 million Americans currently have Alzheimer's, and that number is expected to triple to more than 13 million by 2050. Its cause is still unknown, and there is no known cure. See also, **dementia.**

assisted living facility Housing for older people who cannot live on their own but do not need as much care as a **nursing home** provides. People who live in assisted living facilities usually have their own private apartments and receive help with such things as medication management, bathing, and housekeeping. Assisted living facilities are typically very expensive, and government programs such as Medicare and Medicaid do not help pay for them.

baby boomers The 76 million Americans born between 1946 and 1964, following World War II. Boomers are the country's largest demographic group, and their aging will have profound consequences for the country in terms of social services, housing and health care expenditures. The last of the baby boomers will reach age 55 in 2019, and it is estimated that 20 percent of the U.S. population will be over 65 by 2030.

cognitive decline Decline in mental ability.

dementia A progressive decline in mental ability beyond what is expected from normal aging. It is caused by damage or disease in the brain. The areas typically affected are memory, attention, language, and problem solving. In later stages people who have dementia may be quite disoriented. **Alzheimer's disease** is one type of dementia.

elder abuse Any physical, psychological, financial, or sexual mistreatment of an older adult. Also includes neglect, which is the withholding of care or necessities from an individual, and self-neglect, the inability of an elderly person to take care of themselves.

geriatrics The branch of medicine that focuses on older adults and the prevention and treatment of disease and disability in later life.

gerontology The study of the aging process itself.

hospice A philosophy of caring for terminally ill people that is characterized by concern for relieving symptoms and pain, increasing general well-being, and providing spiritual comfort for those who are dying. See also, **palliative care**.

instrumental activities of daily living (IADLs) Activities that are not necessary for basic self-care, but which are still very important to everyday life. IADLs include the ability to use a telephone, prepare meals, shop for food and clothing, do housework, use transportation, and handle financial matters. See also, **activities of daily living (ADLs)**.

long-term care (LTC) A wide range of supports and services provided to individuals who are unable to live independently because of chronic illness or disability. Although LTC may be provided in a person's home, when most people speak of long-term care, they are referring to **nursing homes**.

means test A requirement that a person must fall below a certain income or asset level to qualify for a government benefit program such as Medicaid or Supplemental Security Income (SSI).

nursing home Any residential facility that provides some degree of medical care to residents. There are three levels of care: skilled, intermediate, and extended. A **skilled nursing facility** offers a full range of medical treatment and personal care to residents. An intermediate care facility offers health-related care for patients who need a lower level of assistance. An extended care facility is primarily a transitional or rehabilitation facility that offers short-term convalescence after a hospital stay.

Older Americans Act (OAA) A 1965 federal law that authorized and established funding for a wide variety of direct services for older adults, such as senior centers, nutrition programs, case management, and information and referral programs.

Olmstead **decision** A landmark 1999 Supreme Court ruling that interpreted the Americans with Disabilities Act (ADA) to mean that elderly and disabled individuals should be allowed to live in the least restrictive setting possible. The *Olmstead* decision has caused a shift away from the institutionalization of the elderly and toward more home-based care.

palliative care Any type of medical care that focuses on reducing the severity of pain and slowing the progress of disease rather than trying to cure it. The goal of palliative care—sometimes also called "comfort care"—is to improve the quality of life rather than prolong it. See also, **hospice**.

skilled nursing facility (SNF) A residential care facility for people who require constant medical attention, but at a lower level of care than a hospital. Usually the residents are elderly, but younger people who need skilled medical care often reside there as well. About 80 percent of skilled nursing facilities in the United States are run by for-profit companies. See also, **nursing home**.

Organizations to Contact

AARP
601 E St. NW, Washington, DC 20049
(800) 424-3410
e-mail: member@aarp.org
Web site: www.aarp.org

AARP, formerly known as the American Association of Retired Persons, is a nonpartisan association that seeks to improve the aging experience for all Americans. It is committed to the preservation of Social Security and Medicare. AARP publishes the magazine *Modern Maturity* and the newsletter *AARP Bulletin*. Issue statements and congressional testimony can be found at the Web site.

Administration on Aging (AOA)
330 Independence Ave. SW
  Washington, DC 20201
(202) 619-0724 • fax: (202) 357-3555
e-mail: aoainfo@aoa.gov
Web site: www.aoa.dhhs.gov

The AOA works with a number of organizations, senior centers, and local service providers to help older people remain independent. It also works to protect the rights of the elderly, prevent crime and violence against older persons, and investigate health care fraud. AOA's publications include fact sheets on issues such as age discrimination, elder abuse, and Alzheimer's disease, many of which are available on its Web site. Additional publications are available through AOA's National Aging Information Center, located at www.aoa.dhhs.gov/naic.

The Alzheimer's Association
919 North Michigan Ave., Suite 1100
  Chicago, IL 60611-1676

(800) 272-3900 • fax: (312) 335-1110
e-mail: info@alz.org
Web site: www.alz.org

The Alzheimer's Association is committed to finding a cure for Alzheimer's and helping those affected by the disease. The association funds research into the causes and treatments of Alzheimer's disease and provides education and support for people diagnosed with the condition, their families, and caregivers. Position statements and fact sheets are available on its Web site.

American Geriatrics Society (AGS)
350 Fifth Ave., Suite 801
  New York, NY 10118
(212) 308-1414 • fax: (212) 832-8646
e-mail: info@americangeriatrics.org
Web site: www.americangeriatrics.org

The American Geriatrics Society is a professional organization of health care providers that aims to improve the health and well-being of all older adults. AGS helps shape attitudes, policies, and practices regarding health care for older people. The society's publications include the book *The American Geriatrics Society's Complete Guide to Aging and Health*, the magazines *Journal of the American Geriatrics Society* and *Annals of Long-Term Care: Clinical Care and Aging*, and *The AGS Newsletter*, recent issues of which are available on its Web site.

American Society on Aging
833 Market St., Suite 511
  San Francisco, CA 94103-1824
(415) 974-9600 • fax: (415) 974-0300
e-mail: info@asaging.org
Web site: www.asaging.org

The American Society on Aging is an organization of health care and social service professionals, researchers, educators, businesspersons, senior citizens, and policy makers that is concerned with all aspects of aging and works to enhance the well-being of older individuals. Its publications include the bi-monthly newspaper *Aging Today* and the quarterly journal *Generations*.

Cato Institute

1000 Massachusetts Ave. NW
  Washington, DC 20001-5403
(202) 842-0200 • fax: (202) 842-3490
e-mail: cato@cato.org
Web site: www.cato.org

The Cato Institute is a libertarian public policy research foundation dedicated to limiting the control of government and protecting individual liberties. Its Project on Social Security seeks to develop a viable plan for privatizing the Social Security system. In addition to the project, the institute provides books, articles, and studies about Social Security on its Web site, as well as articles and studies that support reforming Medicare. The Cato Institute publishes the magazines *Regulation* and *Cato Journal*.

Family Caregiver Alliance (FCA)

80 Montgomery St., Suite 1100
  San Francisco, CA 94104
(800) 445-8106 • fax: (415) 434-3508
e-mail: info@caregiver.org
Web site: www.caregiver.org

Founded in 1977, Family Caregiver Alliance is a community-based nonprofit organization that serves the needs of families and friends providing long-term care at home. FCA offers programs at the national, state, and local levels to support and assist caregivers, and is a public voice for caregivers through education, services, research, and advocacy. Its Web site offers a wide range of information on caregiver issues and resources, including numerous fact sheets, policy papers, and other publications.

International Federation on Ageing (IFA)
425 Viger Ave. W, Suite 520
 Montreal,, Quebec H2Z 1X2 Canada
(514) 396-3358 • fax: (514) 396-3378
e-mail: ifa@citenet.net
Web site: www.ifa-fiv.org

The International Federation on Ageing is a private nonprofit organization that brings together over 150 associations that represent or serve older persons in fifty-four nations. IFA is committed to ensuring the dignity and empowerment of older persons. It publishes the quarterly journal *Ageing International,* and the monthly newsletter *Intercom.*

Medicare Rights Center (MRC)
1460 Broadway, 17th Fl.
 New York, NY 10036
(212) 869-3850 • fax: (212) 869-3532
e-mail: info@medicarerights.org
Web site: www.medicarerights.org

The Medicare Rights Center is a national organization that helps ensure that older adults receive quality affordable health care. It publishes a wide variety of Medicare materials, including a series of self-help pamphlets on Medicare issues and numerous booklets on Medicare-related topics.

National Association for Home Care (NAHC)
228 Seventh St. SE
 Washington, DC 20003
(202) 547-7424 • fax: (202) 547-3540
e-mail: pr@nahc.org
Web site: www.nahc.org

The National Association for Home Care believes that Americans should receive health care and social services in their own homes. It represents home care agencies, hospices, and home care aide organizations. NAHC publishes the quarterly newspaper *Homecare News* and the monthly magazine *Caring.*

National Association of Area Agencies on Aging (N4A)
1730 Rhode Island Ave. NW, Suite 1200
  Washington, DC 20036
(202) 872-0888 • fax: (202) 872-0057
Web site: www.n4a.org

The National Association of Area Agencies on Aging is the umbrella organization for the 655 area agencies on aging in the United States. Its mission is to help older people and those with disabilities live with dignity and choices in their homes and communities for as long as possible. The N4A Web site provides links to Area Agencies on Aging in all states as well as to other government organizations that serve seniors. It also acts as a portal for the Eldercare Locator, a national toll-free number to assist older people and their families find community services for seniors anywhere in the country.

National Center on Elder Abuse (NCEA)
1201 Fifteenth St. NW, Suite 350
  Washington, DC 20005
(202) 898-2586 • fax: (202) 898-2583
e-mail: ncea@nasua.org
Web site: www.elderabusecenter.org

The National Center on Elder Abuse is a gateway to resources on elder abuse, neglect, and exploitation. The NCEA is funded by the U.S. Administration on Aging. The center offers news and resources; collaborates on research; provides consultation, education, and training; identifies and provides information about promising practices and interventions; answers inquiries and requests for information; operates a list-serve forum for professionals; and advises on program and policy development.

National Citizens' Coalition for Nursing Home Reform (NCCNHR)
1424 Sixteenth St. NW, Suite 202
  Washington, DC 20036-2211
(202) 332-2275 • fax: (202) 332-2949

e-mail: nccnhr@nccnhr.org
Web site: www.nccnhr.org

The National Citizens' Coalition for Nursing Home Reform provides information and leadership on federal and state regulatory and legislative policy development and strategies to improve nursing home care and life for residents. Publications include the book *Nursing Homes: Getting Good Care There*, NCCNHR's newsletter *Quality Care Advocate*, and fact sheets on issues such as abuse and neglect, restraints use, and how to choose a nursing home.

National Committee to Preserve Social Security and Medicare
10 G St. NE, Suite 600
   Washington, DC 20004
(800) 966-1935 • fax: (202) 216-0451
e-mail: general@ncpssm.org
Web site: www.ncpssm.org

The National Committee to Preserve Social Security and Medicare is a nonprofit, nonpartisan membership organization. Through advocacy, education, services, and grassroots efforts, the committee works to ensure a secure retirement for all Americans. Its Web site is a good place to find information and analyses regarding Social Security, Medicare, and other retirement issues.

National Council on the Aging (NCOA)
300 D St. SW, Suite 801
   Washington, DC 20024
(202) 479-1200 • fax: (202) 479-0735
e-mail: info@ncoa.org
Web site: www.ncoa.org

The National Council on the Aging is an association of organizations and professionals dedicated to promoting the dignity, self-determination, well-being, and contributions of older people. It advocates business practices, societal attitudes, and public policies that promote vital aging. NCOA's quarterly magazine, *Journal of the National Council on the Aging*, provides tools and insights for community service organizations.

National Hospice and Palliative Care Organization (NHPCO)
1700 Diagonal Rd., Suite 625
  Alexandria, VA 22314
(703) 837-1500 • fax: (703) 837-1233
e-mail: nhpco_info@nhpco.org
Web site: www.nhpco.org

The NHPCO (originally the National Hospice Organization) was founded in 1978 to educate the public about the benefits of hospice care for the terminally ill and their families. It seeks to promote the idea that with the proper care and pain medication, the terminally ill can live out their lives comfortably and in the company of their families. The organization opposes euthanasia and assisted suicide. It conducts educational and training programs for administrators and caregivers in numerous aspects of hospice care. The NHPCO publishes grief and bereavement guides, brochures such as *Hospice Care: A Consumer's Guide to Selecting a Hospice Program* and *Communicating Your End-of-Life Wishes*, and the book *Hospice Care: A Celebration*.

Senior Action in a Gay Environment (SAGE)
305 Seventh Ave., 16th Fl.
  New York, NY 10001
(212) 741-2247 • fax: (212) 366-1947
e-mail: sageusa@aol.com
Web site: www.sageusa.org

Senior Action in a Gay Environment is the world's largest and oldest organization devoted specifically to meeting the needs of aging LGBT (lesbian, gay, bisexual, and transgendered) people. SAGE provides direct services to LGBT seniors in New York City and works to increase awareness of gay aging through education and advocacy throughout the United States.

The Seniors Coalition
9001 Braddock Rd., Suite 200
  Springfield, VA 22151
(703) 239-1960 • fax: (703) 239-1985
e-mail: tsc@senior.org
Web site: www.senior.org

The Seniors Coalition, which positions itself as an alternative to AARP, is a nonpartisan education and issue advocacy organization that represents the concerns of America's senior citizens. Its goals include protecting the Social Security Trust Fund and saving Medicare from bankruptcy. On its Web site the coalition publishes news, articles, and fact sheets on prescription drugs, health, social security, and other issues of concern to seniors.

Bibliography

Books

Stuart Altman and David Shactman	*Policies for an Aging Society.* New York: Johns Hopkins University Press, 2002.
Dean Baker and Mark Weisbrot	*Social Security—the Phony Crisis.* Chicago: University of Chicago Press, 2001.
Sue Blevins	*Medicare's Midlife Crisis.* Washington, DC: Cato Institute, 2001.
Ira Byock	*Dying Well—Peace and Possibilities at the End of Life.* New York: Riverhead, 1998.
Ken Dychtwald	*Age Power—How the 21st Century Will Be Ruled by the New Old.* New York: Penguin Putnam, 1999.
Lita Epstein	*The Complete Idiot's Guide to Social Security.* 1st ed. Indianapolis, IN: Alpha, 2002.
Margaret Morganroth Gullette	*Aged by Culture.* Chicago: University of Chicago Press, 2004.
Jacob S. Hacker	*The Great Risk Shift.* New York: Oxford University Press, 2005.
Mary Hird	*Elder Abuse, Neglect, and Maltreatment: What Can Be Done to Stop It.* Pittsburgh: Dorrance, 2003.

Robert B. Hudson   *The New Politics of Old Age Policy.* New York: Johns Hopkins University Press, 2005.

Harry Moody   *Aging: Concepts and Controversies.* 3rd ed. Thousand Oaks, CA: Pine Forge, 2000.

Daniel Shaviro   *Who Should Pay for Medicare?* Chicago: University of Chicago Press, 2004.

Patricia Smith et al.   *Alzheimer's for Dummies.* Hoboken, NJ: Wiley, 2003.

Michael Tanner   *Social Security and Its Discontents— Perspectives on Choice.* Washington, DC: Cato Institute, 2004.

Rachelle Zukerman   *Eldercare for Dummies.* 1st ed. Hoboken, NJ: Wiley 2003.

Periodicals

Edmund Andrews   "Economic View: Social Security Reform, with One Big Catch," *New York Times*, December 12, 2004.

Associated Press   "Democrats Say Medicare Law Could Eat into Social Security Benefits," *Boston Herald*, July 21, 2004.

Robert M. Ball   "How to Fix Social Security? It Doesn't Have to Be Hard," *Aging Today*, March/April 2004.

Wendy Bonafazi   "Who Pays for Long Term Care?" *Contemporary Long Term Care*, October 1998.

James J. Callahan Jr. | "Giving the Elderly Options on Independent Living," *Boston Globe*, November 24, 2002.

Ken Dychtwald | "Wake Up Call—the 10 Physical, Social, Spiritual, Economic, and Political Crises the Boomers Will Face as They Age in the 21st Century," American Society on Aging, 1997. www.asaging.org

Robert B. Friedland | "Caregivers and Long-Term Care Needs in the 21st Century: Will Public Policy Meet the Challenge?" Issue Brief, Long-Term Care Financing Project, Georgetown University, Washington, DC, 2004.

Victor Fuchs | "Health Care for the Elderly: How Much? Who Will Pay for It?" *Health Affairs*, January/February 1999.

Vicki Haddock | "Seniors Can't Go Home Again—Medi-Cal Rules Force State's Elderly into Costly Nursing Facilities," *San Francisco Chronicle*, August 1, 2004.

Health Policy Institute | "Medicaid and an Aging Population," Fact Sheet, Long-Term Care Financing Project, Georgetown University, Washington, DC, 2004.

Marsha King | "Concerns of Elder Gays—Aging Poses New Healthcare, Legal Challenges for Partners," *Seattle Times*, October 7, 2001.

N.R. Kleinfield | "Lillian and Julia—a Twilight of Fear: Bowed by Age and Battered by an

Addicted Nephew," *New York Times*, December 12, 2004.

Paul Krugman   "Inventing a Crisis," *New York Times*, December 7, 2004.

Michael Lemonick and Alice Park-Mankato   "The Nun Study—How One Scientist and 678 Sisters Are Helping Unlock the Secrets of Alzheimer's," *Time*, May 14, 2001.

Phillip Longman   "Fixing Social Security," *Fortune*, November 1, 2004.

NY Times Editorial Board   "How Not to Save Social Security," *New York Times*, September 23, 2004.

Susanna Schrobsdorff   "The Final Indignity," *Newsweek*, July 19, 2005.

Barbara Stucki and Janemarie Mulvey   "Can Aging Boomers Avoid Nursing Homes?" *Consumers' Research Magazine*, August 2000.

Shankar Vedantam   "Reagans' Experience Alters Outlook for Alzheimer's Patients," *Washington Post*, June 14, 2004.

Jerald Winakur   "What Are We Going to Do with Dad?" *Washington Post*, August 7, 2005.

Index